THE MAIN THING

Those At The Top Must Help Those At The Bottom

Rick Tidwell

Sermon To Book
www.sermontobook.com

The Main Thing / Rick Tidwell
ISBN-13: 9780692405086
ISBN-10: 0692405089

"Awesome times 10! This is such a necessary piece for the church! A short, rich treatise focusing on what Jesus considered most important for his followers. Read it and then re-read it!"

—Rodney Lloyd, Apostolic Leader, USA, S. Africa, Nations

"Rick Tidwell gets it. In very conservative circles it feels like compromising. And in very liberal circles it feels like proselytizing. But what Rick describes as "The Main Thing" is true biblical balance—true New Testament Christianity. When sending his Apostles, Jesus said, "Freely you have received; freely give." Rick Tidwell understands that and unfolds it quite well in this book."

—Troy Ray, Executive Director, Halifax Urban Ministries

"Rick doesn't mince words. It is clear that a belief in God calls for a response in our lives that is visibly lived. This is a book for those serious about being a Christian. Christianity is not for armchair spectators but those willing to live the Gospel. The age-old question of Faith and Works is given the proper perspective in the life of a Christian. One can't have one without the other. Pastor Rick is clear what it means to believe in Jesus Christ as Lord and what that belief entails in our lives."

—Rev. Phil Egitto, Pastor, Our Lady of Lourdes Catholic Church, Daytona Beach, FL

"Practical, straight teaching. Rick hits the nail on the head. God gave us the Comforter, the Holy Ghost, not only to be comforted but to also comfort others. This book challenges our hearts!"

—Steve Upshur, Founder, Peacemakers International, Detroit, MI

To the strong: You have accomplished more than any generation in history. Thank you. You have experienced love, beauty, honor and success. You have earned and enjoyed the heavenly possessions of convenience and comfort. May you now find your life's true calling and purpose—in these pages.

To my loving and gorgeous wife Nina of 29 years: May the message of this book continue to give us the unity of mission for another 29 years!

To our sons Rich and Robert: I could not be more proud of you. May you take this gospel to your generation.

To Jesus: You know everything and you have never turned your back on me. May I have the courage and the strength to do the same for the least among us.

CONTENTS

What's The Main Thing?

Something was missing.

I was a successful minister and founding pastor of a church that grew from zero to three hundred and it wasn't enough. I was a successful businessman earning a six-figure income with a bright future and it wasn't enough.

Those at the top must seek out and help those at the bottom.

I had a gorgeous wife who loved me, two beautiful boys, and the perfect home. But I almost threw it all away—because it wasn't enough.

Something was still missing!

I was missing the one thing, the main thing all strong people need to survive: the strong ought to be helping the weak. Those at the top must seek out and help those at the bottom.

This is "The Main Thing." Without this foundation, the strong will fall. They always have.

John Steinbeck put it like this: "We now face the danger, which in the past has been the most destructive to the humans: Success, plenty, comfort and ever-increasing leisure. No dynamic people has ever survived these dangers."

This book was written so that the strong do not fall but rather hear the call, begin to rise up and take their place next to Jesus in serving the "least" among us.

CHAPTER ONE

"Jimmy"

Years ago, I met a young man named Jimmy. He was probably the most negative person I had ever met. Very few people could even tolerate being around him, including my wife.

If we're going to improve ourselves, we have to go through degrees of discomfort.

Whenever he would stop by the house, she would have to leave or go into another room. But it was through my relationship with Jimmy that God taught me one of the greatest lessons of my life.

Before I tell you more about Jimmy, I must first tell you about God's calling on my life to be a minister over thirty years ago, and how uncomfortable it made me feel.

There were times when my nerves were so out of control that my knees would shake, causing my pants to move. I would hide behind pulpits, hoping the crowd wouldn't see. I remember asking God, "Why did you call me to ministry?" It just didn't come naturally.

In this chapter, we will discuss the uncomfortable things in life that we all face. My reasoning for addressing this issue is this: If we're ever going to improve ourselves, we have to go through degrees of discomfort.

Discomfort is actually beneficial to our growth as believers. If we are unwilling to face the uncomfortable experiences in life, how are we ever going to grow and mature in our walk with God?

Let me ask you: What do you do when you're in a situation that makes you feel uncomfortable? Most of us run for the hills, right? We do whatever it takes to remove ourselves from anything or anyone that causes us discomfort. Our nature is automatically opposed to discomfort. We avoid it at all cost.

But discomfort is actually beneficial to our growth as believers. If we are unwilling to face the uncomfortable experiences in life, how are we ever going to grow and mature in our walk with God?

Did you know that forty percent of eagles die during their first flight? Imagine yourself as an eagle. You're safely in your nest, and one of your friends decides to fly for the first time, only to discover that the attempt was unsuccessful. How would that make you feel? Horrible, right? Life is not much different. It teaches us that if we're ever going to leave the nest (i.e. grow, improve, mature), we have to make decisions to overcome our fears and embrace the uncomfortable moments.

Just the fact that you're reading this book proves that you have an interest in growth and improvement. Keep in mind that there is no improvement in your walk with the Lord without experiencing discomfort.

As followers of Jesus, we must learn to embrace the uncomfortable things in life.

As followers of Jesus, we must learn to embrace the uncomfortable things in life. We must realize that when it comes to growing spiritually, the feelings associated with discomfort are not the enemy. They are *necessary* if we are ever going to mature.

As a minister of the gospel, I am faced with a dilemma: God has given me a gift to teach the words of Jesus and help others grow spiritually, but if my teachings don't spur people to grow, then I have failed.

My purpose in life is to help God's people mature. It's a wonderful purpose and I would not change it for the world. But the truth is that as a teacher speaking the words of Jesus, I am going to make others feel uncomfortable.

Throughout the Bible, it's evident that Jesus made people uncomfortable, too, and He continues to do so today. We all agree that the scriptures say God is a God of comfort, yet there are moments throughout Jesus' ministry when His words caused others to feel uncomfortable—including his own disciples.

3 Examples of Jesus Making Others Uncomfortable

1) One day Jesus said to Peter, "Get thee behind me Satan." How do you think that would make you feel? I don't think you'd be jumping for joy after hearing Jesus speak to you that way. On the contrary! His words would cause you to feel great discomfort.

2) When Jesus came to the temple and discovered the people buying and selling merchandise, he took a whip, turned over their tables, and called them all a "den of thieves". This kind of reaction was out of character for Jesus. His followers knew He was a very kind and compassionate man. But that day, they saw a different side of Him. What He did caused everyone to feel very uncomfortable.

3) As Jesus was talking to the Pharisees, they began to ask Him questions, and His response was, "You're a bunch of snakes." How many of you can agree that those words were very difficult to hear?

We can all be thankful for what Jesus did for us and enjoy the comfort that God has given to His people. But we must also understand that if all we do is live in comfort day after day, we won't grow spiritually. The only way we can improve is by facing (rather than running from) uncomfortable situations.

Today, there are well-known voices in the body of Christ that speak only about the comforting things of God. Yes, we need to hear about God's comfort, but too often such messages produce what I call "comfort junkies".

If we ever want to grow spiritually, we must allow God to teach us things that cause us to be uncomfortable.

If we ever want to grow spiritually, we must allow God to teach us things that cause us to be uncomfortable. John 6:53-66 says:

"Jesus said to them, 'Very truly I tell you, unless you eat the flesh of the Son of Man and drink his blood, you have no life in you. Whoever eats my flesh and drinks my blood has eternal life, and I will raise them up at the last day. For my flesh is real food and my blood is real drink. Whoever eats my flesh and drinks my blood remains in me, and I in them. Just as the living Father sent me and I live because of the Father, so the one who feeds on me will live because of me. This is the bread that came down from heaven. Your ancestors ate manna and died, but whoever feeds on this bread will live forever.' He said this while teaching in the synagogue in Capernaum. On hearing it, many of his disciples said, 'This is a hard teaching. Who can accept it?' Aware that his disciples were grumbling about this, Jesus said to them, 'Does this offend you? Then what if you see the

Son of Man ascend to where he was before! The Spirit gives life; the flesh counts for nothing. The words I have spoken to you—they are full of the Spirit and life. Yet there are some of you who do not believe.' For Jesus had known from the beginning which of them did not believe and who would betray him. He went on to say, 'This is why I told you that no one can come to me unless the Father has enabled them.' From this time many of his disciples turned back and no longer followed him."

We can learn to stand and embrace the discomfort.

Biblical examples such as this prove that when we are faced with the uncomfortable, we will leave. But it doesn't have to be this way. We can learn to stand and embrace the discomfort. This is true in my life. There are times when Jesus speaks words of comfort and times when He says things that cause me to run and hide. To this day, I am learning to embrace the uncomfortable and allow His words to bring change and improvement to my life.

Allow me to share with you a couple of my own experiences in facing discomfort. But before I do, let's take a look at what Jesus says in Luke 5:38-39: "New wine must be stored in new wineskins. But no one who drinks the old wine seems to want the new wine. 'The old is just fine,' they say."

Can you see what He is saying in this verse? It's just like the eagle sitting in his nest, that thinks, *This is just fine. I've seen my friends jump out and plummet to their death, so I am going to stay right here where it's comfortable and safe.*

There is no growth unless we embrace discomfort and jump out of our nest.

It is no different when it comes to human nature. There is no growth unless we embrace discomfort and jump out of our nest. There is no change unless we take a step and move out of our comfort zone.

Jesus says that if we want to change and grow, we must be willing to experience some discomfort. We cannot put new wine into old wineskins without going through some level of discomfort.

Fourteen years ago, God shared something with me that made me very uncomfortable. Yet when I embraced it, everything about my life improved. Had I run from what God taught me, I would not be the same person today.

Anyone who knows me will tell you that I'm a changed man. Not only did my life change, but my family also changed. Together we are in a better place, spiritually, because of what the Lord revealed to me.

The Day Everything Changed for Me

One evening while sitting in my living room, Jesus came into the room. I did not see Him in a physical sense, but I knew His presence was there. We had just moved back to our hometown after living in Arizona, where I had always been very successful in business. It seemed as though everything I touched turned to gold. Yet when we arrived back home, I literally had only fourteen dollars left in my pocket with no credit, no prospects, and no interviews. To top it off, I had a family to support. I found myself in the middle of my life with nothing to show for it. If you want a true definition of what it feels like to be uncomfortable, that was it!

This is not a parable. This is not a story. This is going to happen one day.

Even though I did not see or hear Jesus, His presence was more powerful than any experience I have ever had in my entire life. At that moment the Spirit of God said, "Open your Bible to Mathew 25." Now, I had been a Bible student most of my Christian life and had read the entire Bible many times. Page after page was marked, highlighted, and underlined, and I had an answer for everything.

But when I opened to that chapter, there wasn't a mark in it. It was as if it had never existed. He then said, "This is not a parable. This is not a story. This is going to happen one day."

Mathew 25:31-46 says, "When the Son of Man comes in his glory, and all the angels with him, he will sit on his glorious throne. All the nations will be gathered before him, and he will separate the people one from another as a shepherd separates the sheep from the goats. He will put the sheep on his right and the goats on his left.

"Then the King will say to those on his right, 'Come, you who are blessed by my Father; take your inheritance, the kingdom prepared for you since the creation of the world. For I was hungry and you gave me something to eat, I was thirsty and you gave me something to drink, I was a stranger and you invited me in, I needed clothes and you clothed me, I was sick and you looked after me, I was in prison and you came to visit me.'

Depart from me, you who are cursed, into the eternal fire prepared for the devil and his angels. For I was hungry and you gave me nothing to eat.

"Then the righteous will answer him, 'Lord, when did we see you hungry and feed you, or thirsty and give you something to drink? When did we see you a stranger and invite you in, or needing clothes and clothe you? When did we see you sick or in prison and go to visit you?'

"The King will reply, 'Truly I tell you, whatever you did for one of the least of these brothers and sisters of mine, you did for me.'

"Then he will say to those on his left, 'Depart from me, you who are cursed, into the eternal fire prepared for the devil and his angels. For I was hungry and you gave me nothing to eat, I was thirsty and you gave me nothing to drink, I was a stranger and you did not invite me in, I needed clothes and you did not clothe me, I was sick and in prison and you did not look after me.'

"They also will answer, 'Lord, when did we see you hungry or thirsty or a stranger or needing clothes or sick or in prison, and did not help you?'

"He will reply, 'Truly I tell you, whatever you did not do for one of the least of these, you did not do for me.'

"Then they will go away to eternal punishment, but the righteous to eternal life."

Then Jesus said, "I'm not talking to you about the things that you are already doing. I'm talking to you about what you're not doing."

As I read the verse about refusing to help the least of these, it was as if Jesus was speaking directly to me. Remember what I said earlier? Our nature is to avoid discomfort at all cost. After hearing Jesus speak to me, I wanted to run for the hills. My next thought was, "Why don't we just go to Mathew 26 or 27. Let's just go to the verse that says, "Go into all the world and preach the gospel"?

Then Jesus said, "I'm not talking to you about the things that you are already doing. I'm talking to you about what you're not doing. There is an omission that you're committing. When you refused to help the least of these, you were refusing to help me. And they will go into eternal punishment, but the righteous will go into eternal life."

Wouldn't you agree that the words of Jesus in this chapter could make us feel uncomfortable? To this day, those words make me uncomfortable. We need to remember that the same Jesus who said, "Come to me and I will give you rest" also spoke the words recorded in Mathew 25:31-46.

So what do we do? I believe that one of the reasons Jesus came into my living room that day was to call me to teach what He revealed to me that day. It's not what we *are* doing. Jesus is drawing our attention to what we're *not* doing.

> *Do you love yourself enough to wear clothes? Do you love yourself enough to make sure you have shelter? Jesus said if you're going to be a Christian, you need to love your neighbor the same way.*

If all I do is teach the "comfortable" things, then there is no change, no improvement. We need to take a good look at what He is telling us and begin to do them. The Bible says, "Be not hearers only, but doers of the word of God." We need to *show* our world that we are true followers of Jesus. They've heard our words. It is time that they see who He is by our *actions*. Remember what Jesus said in the story of the Good Samaritan? "Go and do likewise."

Our oldest son, who recently preached at our church, said it this way, "Everyone knows that we are to love our neighbor as we love ourselves. If that's true, do you make sure you love yourself enough to drink water every day? Do you make sure that you love yourself enough to eat food? Do you love yourself enough to wear clothes? Do you love yourself enough to make sure you have shelter? Jesus said if you're going to be a Christian, you need to love your neighbor the *same* way." All of this came from the mouth of our 26-year-old son. Even I did not come to learn and understand this truth until I was in my forties!

> *From then on, I was going to treat the least as Jesus and I was going to teach others to do the same.*

As Jesus spoke those words to me through Matthew 25, I began to weep. Everything He said was so real to me. I received my marching orders that day and I knew then what I was going to do the rest of my life. From then on, I was going to treat the least as Jesus and I was going to teach others to do the same.

Remember my friend, Jimmy? He suffered more than any other human being I know. At the age of sixteen, he was in a car accident that effected his blood circulation, causing his legs and ankles to be swollen and discolored, making it very difficult for him to walk.

Prior to the accident, he was full of health and quite athletic. From the age of sixteen until about 40 years old, he suffered every day and could only get around by the use of a cane. After reconnecting with Jimmy over coffee, I started to befriend him and realized that we both attended the same church.

Every time I met with him, he would talk constantly about everything in his life that was wrong. He was not only suffering and in pain, he had also become the most negative person you'd ever meet. In fact, he was the most negative person I had ever met.

Every time we'd meet, he would never say "hello" or "how are you?" Without fail, he would begin talking about anything and everything negative. I remember timing him one day and he went on and on for forty-five minutes.

One day as he began to talk, I looked him right in the eye and said, "Jimmy, I am not going to acknowledge that you even exist until you begin by saying hello to me and ask how I'm doing."

One day as he began to talk, I looked him right in the eye and said, "Jimmy, I am not going to acknowledge that you even exist until you begin by saying hello to me and ask how I'm doing. I'm no longer going to talk to you until you acknowledge that I am also a human being on this earth just like you."

I'm happy to say that instead of being offended, he began to improve. From then on, before each conversation, he greeted me by saying, "Hi Rick, how are you?"

During this time, I had just learned about Mathew 25 and that the "least" is Jesus. According to those verses, I also began to realize that Jimmy is Jesus. He sure didn't look like Jesus, and he certainly did not sound like Jesus. There was nothing about him that even resembled Jesus. He was just Jimmy.

All of this began to take place not long after God had led our family to live in Michigan, where both my wife and I were born and raised. The Lord led us to our new home out of the city on a lake. Even though it was new to us, our house was one hundred years old, originally built to be a vacation cottage. This is the same house in which God revealed Mathew 25 to me.

Not long after my experience with the Lord, I remember sitting in the front yard, enjoying the beautiful view of the lake and soaking up the sunshine.

Not long after my experience with the Lord, I remember sitting in the front yard, enjoying the beautiful view of the lake and soaking up the sunshine. As I looked up, I saw Jimmy coming around the side of the house, walking very slow with his cane. As he approached, the Spirit of God said, "Here comes Jesus."

I said to the Lord, "That's not Jesus. That's Jimmy!" But because the presence of God was so prevalent, I thought, *Well, I'd better just let this play out and see what Jesus has to say today.*

As I sat there, I was expecting Jimmy to come up with something spiritual like a deep revelation and sure enough, he said, "Hi Rick, how are you?" and immediately jumped right into 45 minutes of negative banter.

About half way through, the Spirit of God spoke to me again and said, "That's what you sound like to me. All of your whining and complaining. All of your doubt, worry, fear and cares of this world. All of your money and possessions. That's what you sound like to me!" I must admit, what He said made me very uncomfortable. Why? Because I thought I was better than Jimmy.

Then the Spirit of God spoke to me again and said, "If you'll be merciful to Jimmy, I'll be merciful to you." After the Lord spoke to me, I no longer felt I had a right to stop Jimmy from talking about his troubles and everything that was wrong in his life.

One afternoon, while my wife ran errands, she had to drive right by the hospital where Jimmy was staying. As she approached the cross street, the Spirit of God spoke to her.

As time went by, Jimmy began to change, but in a good way. One afternoon he came with gifts for our two young boys. This is something he would not have done before.

Not long after, the Lord began to speak to my wife and I about moving from Michigan to Florida. A few weeks before we moved, Jimmy went to the hospital. He had been in the hospital many times before, but this would be the last time we would see him.

One afternoon, while my wife ran errands, she had to drive right by the hospital where Jimmy was staying. As she approached the cross street, the Spirit of God spoke to her.

This is her story:

As I was approaching the main road to the hospital where Jimmy was admitted, the Spirit of God spoke to me and said, "Go visit Jimmy." When I heard His voice, I didn't want to do it and resisted it as much as I could.

My next thought was "If I drive past the main road, I just might be able to get out of it." But to no avail. The Spirit of God was persistent because He knew eventually I would listen to His voice and turn the car around, which I ended up doing.

> *During our conversation I could tell that he was a little frightened of the unknown. As we continued our conversation, the presence of God began to fill the room.*

When I entered Jimmy's room, he was awake to greet me. As we began talking, I realized that this visit was different than any other time I had been in the same room as Jimmy.

This day he was very kind and did not say one negative word. During our conversation I could tell that he was a little frightened of the unknown. As we continued our conversation, the presence of God began to fill the room.

It was at that moment that I felt the Lord wanting me to share with him a recent dream I had. In the dream, Jimmy and I were standing outside by a car talking. In the dream, everything was white! The houses were white, the roads were white, even our clothes were white.

I also remember that Jimmy was no longer sick. He was whole and no longer needed the use of his cane. After sharing my dream with him, he asked, "Do you think the dream took place here on earth or in heaven?"

I told him that I did not know for sure, but I thought it was in heaven. When I shared that with him, he began to weep.

> *I felt the Lord lead me to pray with him and it was at this time that I felt a heavenly peace fill the room and I noticed that Jimmy's fear vanished and the peace of God came over him.*

That is when I felt the Lord lead me to pray with him and it was at this time that I felt a heavenly peace fill the room and I noticed that Jimmy's fear vanished and the peace of God came over him. This was the last time I would see Jimmy."

Not too long after leaving Michigan and arriving at our new home in Florida, we received news that Jimmy had gone to be with the Lord. When I heard this news, the Spirit of God spoke to me again and said, "He was never more ready to come to heaven in his whole life, so I took him."

The Lord made me realize that Jimmy's heart was in a good place. He had finally let go of grudges and had forgiven his family. This is what happens when we reach out to the least. The only way we'll ever successfully help them is by remembering that Jesus is the least.

CHAPTER TWO

Idleness

When something is idle, what is it doing? Nothing, right? It's like a car in park with the engine running. Even though the vehicle is able to charge down the road, it's sitting motionless with no obvious purpose.

According to the Bible, the evildoer and the idle person will suffer the same fate.

When it comes to human behavior, living in a state of idleness does not appear to be a bad thing. In fact, it seems quite harmless. Idle people tend to keep to themselves and mind their own business, not bothering anyone. But is that how believers should live?

Let me ask you a question. What seems worse to you, someone committing evil or someone being idle? Most people would agree that evilness is worse than idleness. But according to the Bible, the evildoer and the idle person will suffer the same fate.

Edmund Burke says, "The only thing necessary for the triumph of evil is for good men to do nothing." When good people remain idle, it actually fuels evil. The Bible says that evil is aggressive and seeks to devour (John 10:10).

Bishop Desmond Tutu says, "To be neutral in a situation of injustice is to choose the side of the oppressor." In other words, no response *is* a response.

> *Jesus loves us enough to correct us and point us in the right direction.*

Revelation 3:15 says, "I know all the things you do, that you are neither hot nor cold. I wish you were one or the other! But since you are like lukewarm water, neither hot nor cold, I will spit you out of my mouth! You say, 'I am rich, I have everything I want. I don't need a thing!' And you don't realize that you are wretched and miserable and poor and blind and naked. So I advise you to buy gold from me—gold that has been purified by fire. Then you will be rich."

Jesus is not talking to the world. He is talking to His church. Jesus loves us enough to correct us and point us in the right direction. Verse 20 says, "Look! I stand at the door and knock. If you hear my voice and open the door, I will come in, and we will share a meal together as friends."

When my wife read these verses, she said, "I have heard this message preached time after time. I've even preached it myself, but I did not realize until now that

Jesus is not talking to the unbeliever. He is talking to His church! He is knocking at our door!"

The apostle Paul says, "And now dear brothers and sisters we give you this command in the name of our Lord Jesus Christ: Stay away from all believers who live idle lives and don't follow the tradition they received from us" (2 Thessalonians 3:6-8).

He is commanding His church to stay away from believers who are idle, lukewarm and indifferent.

If you notice, Jesus is not saying to stay away from sinners. The scriptures tell us that He Himself sat and dined with them. He is commanding His church to stay away from believers who are idle, lukewarm and indifferent.

Idleness is contagious, and thus, can rub off on other believers. Verses 11-15 say, "Yet we hear that some of you are living idle lives, refusing to work and meddling in other people's business. We command such people and urge them in the name of the Lord Jesus Christ to settle down and work to earn their own living. As for the rest of you, dear brothers and sisters, never get tired of doing good. Take note of those who refuse to obey what we say in this letter. Stay away from them so they will be ashamed. Don't think of them as enemies, but warn them as you would a brother or sister."

Over fourteen years ago, when God opened my eyes to the truths in Matthew 25:31-46 regarding the fate of those who refused to help the least of these, I had difficulty believing it. In those verses, Jesus doesn't address the "big" sins that we as a church normally condemn. Instead, he condemned the sin of idleness.

> *As Christians, we think we're connecting to Jesus during our celebrations on Sunday mornings. This has some truth, but Jesus says we connect with Him when we love our neighbor and help the least of these.*

As Christians, we think we're connecting to Jesus during our celebrations on Sunday mornings. This has some truth, but in Matthew 25, Jesus says we connect with Him when we love our neighbor and help the least of these.

Matthew 25:44-45 says, "Then they will reply, 'Lord, when did we ever see you hungry or thirsty or a stranger or naked or sick or in prison, and not help you?' And he will answer, 'I tell you the truth, when you refused to help the least of these, you were refusing to help me.'"

If we're not helping the least Monday through Saturday, I'm not sure God is happy with us on Sunday. Jesus tells us in chapter 25 that the idle, the evil, and Satan himself will suffer the same fate: "And they will go away into eternal punishment, but the righteous will go into eternal life" (Matthew 25:46).

Jesus teaches the same principle in Luke 16, regarding the rich man and the poor beggar.

Luke 16:19-31 says, "Jesus said, 'There was a certain rich man who was splendidly clothed in purple and fine linen and who lived each day in luxury. At his gate lay a

poor man named Lazarus who was covered with sores.
As Lazarus lay there longing for scraps from the rich
man's table, the dogs would come and lick his open
sores.

*Son, remember that during your lifetime
you had everything you wanted, and
Lazarus had nothing. So now he is here
being comforted, and you are in anguish.*

Finally, the poor man died and was carried by the
angels to be with Abraham. The rich man also died and
was buried, and his soul went to the place of the
dead. There, in torment, he saw Abraham in the far
distance with Lazarus at his side. The rich man shouted,
'Father Abraham, have some pity! Send Lazarus over
here to dip the tip of his finger in water and cool my
tongue. I am in anguish in these flames.' But Abraham
said to him, 'Son, remember that during your lifetime
you had everything you wanted, and Lazarus had
nothing. So now he is here being comforted, and you are
in anguish. And besides, there is a great chasm
separating us. No one can cross over to you from here,
and no one can cross over to us from there.' Then the
rich man said, 'Please, Father Abraham, at least send
him to my father's home. For I have five brothers, and I
want him to warn them so they don't end up in this place
of torment.' But Abraham said, 'Moses and the prophets
have warned them. Your brothers can read what they
wrote.' The rich man replied, 'No, Father Abraham! But
if someone is sent to them from the dead, then they will

repent of their sins and turn to God.' But Abraham said, 'If they won't listen to Moses and the prophets, they won't listen even if someone rises from the dead.'"

> *To flee from being a lukewarm or idle Christian, take the first ten percent of what God gives you and remove poverty with it.*

In today's society, we make up our own convenient excuses to avoid helping others. To flee from being a lukewarm or idle Christian, take the first ten percent of what God gives you and remove poverty with it. Tithing is for the poor.

Deuteronomy 14:22,27-29 says, "You must set aside a tithe of your crops—one-tenth of all the crops you harvest each year...And do not neglect the Levites in your town, for they will receive no allotment of land among you...At the end of every third year, bring the entire tithe of that year's harvest and store it in the nearest town. Give it to the Levites, who will receive no allotment of land among you, as well as to the foreigners living among you, the orphans, and the widows in your towns, so they can eat and be satisfied. Then the Lord your God will bless you in all your work."

God never ordained that the first ten percent should go toward building churches, nor to be used for making big productions on Sunday mornings.

From the very beginning, tithing was ordained by God to remove poverty in the earth. The scriptures prove that when the first ten percent is used correctly, it causes the blessing of God to come to any person, any family, any country and any church.

Abraham practiced this, and the first ten percent went to Melchizedek, who was a priest and this was to be instituted and put in place forever, and that the tenth was to go toward helping the poor.

The scriptures reveal: The first ten percent was always for the poor.

Deuteronomy 14:10 says, "Give generously to the poor, not grudgingly, for the Lord your God will bless you in everything you do."

The scriptures don't lie. The first ten percent should go to the poor. If your church is not using the first ten percent to help the poor, I encourage you to give directly to the poor. Or find a church that does.

Ezekiel 44:28 says, "The priest will not have any property or possession of land..." Moses said that as well. The priests are to live off the offerings of the people. He's to give himself to the service of God, to prayer and to the ministry of the Word.

Ezekiel 44:29 says, "Their food will come from the gifts and sacrifices brought to the temple by the people. The grain offerings, the sin offerings, the guilt offerings. Whatever anyone sets apart for the Lord will belong to the priest. The first of the ripe fruits and all the gifts brought to the Lord will go to the priest. The first samples of each grain harvest and the first of your flour must also be given to the priest, so the Lord will bless your home." The people were to bring the first ten percent to the Priest and he was to distribute it among the priests, widows, orphans and strangers in need.

In Acts, the people of God gave abundantly to remove poverty and relieve human suffering. The apostles testified powerfully to the resurrection of the Lord Jesus, and God's great blessing was upon them all. There were no needy people among them, because those who owned land or houses would sell them and bring the money to the apostles to give to those in need (Acts 4:32-35).

> *Jesus emphasizes the importance of giving gifts to the poor. He is also warning His people to show love toward God by loving our neighbor and helping those in need.*

Their giving went well beyond ten percent. But remember, ten percent is a good start to move us out of idleness. Luke 11:39-42 says, "Then the Lord said to him, 'You Pharisees are so careful to clean the outside of the cup and the dish, but inside you are filthy—full of greed and wickedness! Fools! Didn't God make the inside as well as the outside? So clean the inside by giving gifts to the poor, and you will be clean all over. What sorrow awaits you Pharisees! For you are careful to tithe even the tiniest income from your herb gardens, but you ignore justice and the love of God. You should tithe, yes, but do not neglect the more important things.'"

Here, Jesus emphasizes the importance of giving gifts to the poor. He is also warning His people to show love toward God by loving our neighbor and helping those in need.

In Matthew 6:21 Jesus says, "For where your treasure is, there will your heart be also." Are we giving our first ten percent to God to help humanity? If we are, this is proof that our heart is connected to God.

"And I will give them singleness of heart and put a new spirit within them. I will take away their stony, stubborn heart and give them a tender, responsive heart, so they will obey my decrees and regulations. Then they will truly be my people, and I will be their God" (Ezekiel 11:19-20).

Twenty-four hours a day, He would get up and relieve human suffering one person at a time.

If we look at the life of Jesus, we see that He was moved with compassion. Twenty-four hours a day, He would get up and relieve human suffering one person at a time.

Zechariah 7:8-11 says, "Then this message came to Zechariah from the Lord: 'This is what the Lord of Heaven's Armies says: Judge fairly, and show mercy and kindness to one another. Do not oppress widows, orphans, foreigners, and the poor. And do not scheme against each other. Your ancestors refused to listen to this message. They stubbornly turned away and put their fingers in their ears to keep from hearing. They made their hearts as hard as stone, so they could not hear the instructions or the messages that the Lord of heaven's armies had sent them by his Spirit through the earlier prophets.'"

So what does it mean to be hard-hearted? It means to be stubborn and refuse to help the poor and those who are suffering. This is what it means to be idle.

The new heart that God gives us is one that learns to do good and seeks justice.

Wash yourselves and be clean!
   Get your sins out of my sight.
   Give up your evil ways.
Learn to do good.
   Seek justice.
Help the oppressed.
   Defend the cause of orphans.
   Fight for the rights of widows.

"Come now, let's settle this,"
   says the Lord.
"Though your sins are like scarlet,
   I will make them as white as snow.
Though they are red like crimson,
   I will make them as white as wool.
If you will only obey me,
   you will have plenty..." — **Isaiah 1:16**

The new heart that God gives us is one that learns to do good and seeks justice. So where do we go from here? I am asking every person reading this book to join God's cause in relieving the oppressed.

We can begin by giving the first ten percent that God gives to us to the poor. By doing this, we are declaring that we refuse to be idle, indifferent, and lukewarm. I do not want to suffer the same fate as the evildoer. I choose to do my part.

THE MAIN THING · 33

Weeds

If you have a yard and you enjoy gardening, what is the best method you use to attack weeds? I would think that most of us pull them out of the ground by their roots. If we try to get rid of them simply by cutting the surface, we'll find that our time is simply wasted.

If we can understand the nature of weeds, we will better understand human behavior.

Of course, they may look better temporarily, but we've done nothing to the weed itself. I recently read an article that said if you leave ten small tentacles in the ground, that weed will produce ten more of its kind. And of course any seeds from that one weed will produce more weeds. If we fail to destroy them at the root, we will cause the weeds to spread.

If we can understand the nature of weeds, we will better understand human behavior. According to the scriptures, human behavior is based on the same principle as weeds. If we can ever understand the nature of a weed, we will be able to deal with our own human behavior.

As we all know, weeds are very easy to grow. In comparison to human behavior, I'm talking about the mistakes we make and the things we do wrong. I'm not sure about you, but for me, I find it's very easy to make mistakes.

> *The good that we omit is the root that produces the bad that we find so easy to do.*

Just like the weed, the things we do that are not good for us are very easy to do. Many times the mistakes we make are very easy to do because they are accompanied with pleasure and oftentimes become habitual.

I've noticed in my own life that it's very easy to doubt. It's very easy to worry and to be afraid and hopeless. It's also very easy to lose faith and become angry and bitter, judge and complain. These life experiences are very easy to fall into just like a weed. They are very easy to grow and are seemingly unstoppable.

This is also true when it comes to human behavior. If we're only working on the surface of the problem—and not tackling it at the root—then it's of no value. There are two components of a mistake: The *visible* part and the *root*. I am going to submit two clarifications of a mistake.

The good that we omit is the root that produces the bad that we find so easy to do. If I'm spending all my time addressing the acts I'm committing, I'm doing nothing about the root. On the surface, I may look better and I may be more acceptable to society, but I am doing nothing about the root cause that is producing the behavior.

Although we all sin in thousands of different ways every day, we all have the same root. Therefore, it's wrong for us to judge one another's weeds.

Just like there are different types of weeds, we all have different sins we commit. Studies show that there are approximately 8,000 varieties of weeds. Human behavior is no different. Although we all sin in thousands of different ways every day, we all have the same root. Therefore, it's wrong for us to judge one another's weeds. Jesus says this is nonsense.

If we want to get rid of our weeds, we must deal with the root first. In Matthew 23:25-26, Jesus says, "...you are so careful to clean the outside of the dish, but inside you are filthy—full of greed and self indulgence! You blind Pharisee! First wash the inside of the cup and the dish, and then the outside will become clean too." It is safe to say that in these verses, Jesus identifies human behavior and in this particular verse, He tells us exactly what the root of their sin is: "Greed and self-indulgence."

In Luke 11:39-40 Jesus says, "You Pharisees are so careful to clean the outside of the cup and the dish, but inside you are filthy—full of greed and wickedness! Fools!"

According to these verses, it's a waste of time and energy and resources to just clean up the outside while ignoring the inside. It is *only* when we attack the root of the plant that the weeds whither and die.

> *Every wrong act that has ever been committed has been forgiven, by God's grace. However, according to the scriptures, there is no mercy for the sins of omission.*

Now that we have this understanding, we can now take our focus off the mistakes of others and focus on our own mistakes. There is a perfect example of this concept in the Bible, and it's something that God revealed to me years ago.

In this story, God pulls back the curtain and tells us what happened at the ancient city of Sodom, and it is very appropriate for our society today.

In Ezekiel 16:50, God is speaking to the prophet, Ezekiel, saying, "Behold, this is the iniquity (sin) of thy sister Sodom…" Now, before I go any further, let me establish that the outward sin of Sodom was sexual perversion.

All we ever hear about is Sodom's outward sin. That's not what we should be focused on. Why? Because every wrong act that has ever been committed has been forgiven, by God's grace.

However, according to the scriptures, there is no mercy for the sins of "omission". Think about that for a moment. There is no mercy for the good deeds that we omit. So we'd better get busy finding out what it is we've been omitting.

The world and religion focus on the wrongful committed acts, yet God doesn't pay any attention to them! All He sees is the blood of Jesus and the forgiveness of sin, but He does hold us accountable for the good we're not doing.

The wicked are too proud to seek God; they seem to think that God is dead.

The modern church has not taught us this message regarding the sins of "omission". The Bible does. When God speaks about the real issue of Sodom, He's addressing the "inside" of the cup, the root. He's looking at the cause that's producing their wrongful acts. Jesus Himself said that the generation He lived in was worse than the generation of Sodom. Why? They saw Jesus and would not do what He said.

It's one thing to hear what your spouse says and not do it, but to hear *Jesus* and continue to sin, Lord have mercy.

In Ezekiel 16:50, the first thing God addresses is pride. Psalm 10:4 says, "The wicked are too proud to seek God; they seem to think that God is dead."

Psalm 10:2-3 says, "The wicked arrogantly hunt down the poor...for they brag about their evil desires; they praise the greedy and curse the Lord." In these verses,

God is teaching us not to neglect the poor. God wants us to be aware that there is no mercy if we choose to neglect the poor and allow them to suffer. This is pride, and it is also the root problem. So we see that pride is attached to "doing nothing".

Fullness of Bread

My pantry is full; my refrigerator is full; my bank account is full. God says this is one of the "root" problems of life. He's not talking about having enough for yourself, but what's the context? While others go without. This was the sin of Sodom.

Again, what was the sin of Sodom? Pride, fullness of bread, abundance of idleness, refusing to help others, and accumulating possessions while others were suffering.

James is one of the 5 people who knew Jesus the best. James 5:3 says, "Your gold and silver have become worthless, the very wealth you're counting on will eat away your flesh like fire. This treasure you have accumulated will stand as evidence against you on the day of judgment."

Again, what was the sin of Sodom? Pride, fullness of bread, abundance of idleness, refusing to help others, and accumulating possessions while others were suffering.

At Ponce Church, we have an ongoing, weekly serving of 150 meals to our homeless friends in Daytona

Beach, as well as, a canned food and peanut butter drive in which we donate to local food banks and charities in our area.

This happens every Sunday, week after week, month after month. Even small acts such as this can help to chop away at the "root" problem. Get involved in helping those in need. It can be a local shelter or a food bank. It doesn't matter where you start, but it does matter that you begin to move in that direction.

Their sin of commission wasn't the issue, it was the fact that they did nothing to help the suffering man.

Idleness (i.e. doing nothing while others suffer), was the sin of Sodom and it's also the sin of mankind today. In Matthew 25:31-46, when Jesus is talking about the sheep and the goats on judgment day, the goats are identified by the acts of good that they failed to do.

In the true story of the rich man, he went to hell, and the only sin that was identified was not all his wealth and self-indulgence, but the fact that he never helped the beggar at his gate.

In the story of the Good Samaritan, Jesus called out the sin of the Priest and the Levite who ignored a man lying in the ditch. Their sin of commission wasn't the issue, it was the fact that they did nothing to help the suffering man.

Daniel 4:27 says, "Wherefore, O king, let my counsel be acceptable unto thee, and break off thy sins by righteousness, and thine iniquities by showing mercy to the poor; if it may be a lengthening of thy tranquility."

Begin to increase your level of doing good today. Ask yourself, "What good could I be doing to help those who suffer?" If you do this, God will show you someone in your life whom you could help.

CHAPTER FOUR

Poser

Webster's Dictionary describes the word "poser" as "one who poses". This is not much of a definition, but after more research, I found that a poser is someone who appears to be someone they're not.

There are real bikers, posers, and riders like me, who ride a Suzuki with shorts and sandals.

This is true in the Harley biker world. I'm a rider myself, but I would not consider myself a poser. There are real bikers, posers, and riders like me, who ride a Suzuki with shorts and sandals.

I recently came across a webpage for a Christian motorcycle club and the first thing I read was this: "We are Christian bikers; we are not Christians who ride Harley's." In other words, "Christians who ride Harley's are posers, but we are the real deal!"

Not too long ago, my wife and I were having lunch at our favorite restaurant, which offers indoor and outdoor seating. While I was ordering our food, my wife noticed what I would consider a real biker.

Jesus spent a lot of time exposing posers. He was considered very radical compared to the religious leaders of His generation.

On the back of his jacket, it had a design similar to the Coca-Cola logo and underneath the design it said, "Things go better with Satan." If that's what a real biker is supposed to be, then I would rather be a poser. But in the biker world, you can usually identify real bikers by what they wear, and they are usually really tough looking, having nothing but a Harley.

Then there are the posers who have all the Harley attire and they've invested thousands of dollars to look like a true Harley rider, but most real bikers would consider them posers.

Jesus spent a lot of time exposing posers. In fact, it was a large part of His ministry. He was considered very radical compared to the religious leaders of His generation. This is one of the reasons I fell in love with Jesus. In the 1960s, I was very radical myself and I didn't like the society we were living in.

My generation was all about "down with the man" and we called them "plastic people". To me, you weren't a real person unless your hair was long and you were getting high all the time. To us, anyone who did those things was considered a real person. Now that I am older, I realize that we were posers too.

Matthew 23:27-33 says, "What sorrow awaits you teachers of religious law and you Pharisees. Hypocrites! For you are like whitewashed tombs—beautiful on the outside, but filled on the inside with dead people's bones and all sorts of impurity. Outwardly you look like righteous people, but inwardly your hearts are filled with hypocrisy and lawlessness. Snakes! Sons of vipers! How will you escape the judgment of hell?"

The people He exposed were respected, honored and revered speakers of God.

Those are some very strong words. Can you see here how Jesus took on the religious establishment of His time? Nearly all those in the crowd who heard His words could have very well thought, *What is this guy doing? These people can have you killed today!* The people who heard Jesus must have been blown away by His boldness. Keep in mind, it was not at the end of His ministry that He exposed them. He addressed the religious leaders in His very first sermon, the Sermon on the Mount.

Remember, the people He exposed were respected, honored and revered speakers of God. They were feared and no one appeared to question their authority. And Jesus basically calls them out, saying, "Beware of false prophets who come disguised as harmless sheep but are really vicious wolves. You can identify them by their fruit, that is, by the way they act" (Matthew 7:15-16).

Notice, they are not identified by their words, but by their actions. Let's continue with verse 20, "Yes, just as you can identify a tree by its fruit, so you can identify people by their actions. Not everyone who calls out to me Lord, Lord will enter the Kingdom of Heaven."

Jesus loves everyone, but He is light, and there's no darkness allowed when light shows up.

Jesus loves everyone, but He is light, and there's no darkness allowed when light shows up. There's no hiding, so if there are any secrets, He exposes them.

I cannot stress how much God loves everyone, and when He sent Jesus, He sent Him for everyone. It doesn't matter if you've been the outcast or the leper. It doesn't matter if you've been a glutton or a drunkard, a prostitute or a tax collector. Everyone was, and is, accepted.

Jesus has no problem accepting all people. Oftentimes we make such an issue over our weaknesses, mistakes, and sins, but God doesn't.

However, because He is light, He cannot allow "posing" and will uncover it. Posers and claimers are all welcome, but we must stop posing. Basically, if you claim to be a Christian, you must become a "real" person, because God knows everything about you. And if we are going to have any kind of relationship with Him, we will have to accept who we are, mistakes and all.

Every time Jesus came in contact with posers, He would expose them. I don't know about you, but I don't want to be a "poser". I want to be an authentic Christian, who is doing the will of my heavenly Father.

Even though Judas may have been the most famous poser recorded in the Bible, there are two others who just might be in the same company as him.

Why have you let Satan fill your heart? You lied to the Holy Spirit, and you kept some of the money for yourself.

Acts 5:1 says, "But there was a certain man named Ananias who, with his wife, Sapphira, sold some property. He brought part of the money to the apostles, claiming it was the full amount. With his wife's consent, he kept the rest."

I'm sure most of us know what happened to this couple and I can almost guarantee that the news of what happened to them spread like wildfire. In verse 4, it was revealed to Peter that they had given part of the money but they claimed to give it all. "Then Peter said, "Ananias, why have you let Satan fill your heart? You lied to the Holy Spirit, and you kept some of the money for yourself. The property was yours to sell or not sell, as you wished. And after selling it, the money was also yours to give away. How could you do a thing like this? You weren't lying to us but to God!" As soon as Ananias heard these words, he fell to the floor and died."

Let's look at what happens when the wife comes in looking for Ananias. "About three hours later, his wife came in, not knowing what had happened. Peter asked her, 'Was this the price you and your husband received for your land?' 'Yes,' she replied. 'That was the price.'

And Peter said, 'How could the two of you even think of conspiring to test the Spirit of the Lord like this? The young men who buried your husband are just outside the door, and they will carry you out, too.'

Instantly, she fell to the floor and died."

> *If you want to give a portion, give a portion. If you don't want to give any, don't give any. But no matter what you do, no posing. Don't appear to be one way when you're really something else.*

What did Peter say to them before they died? He told them that the property was theirs to sell or not sell as they wished. Notice, they were still in good standing with God because it was up to them what they wanted to do with the property.

If they decided to sell it, they had the right to give the money away or keep it. What kind of impact did this leave on the people? "Great fear gripped the entire church and everyone else who heard what had happened" (Acts 5:12).

What's the message? If you want to give a portion, give a portion. If you don't want to give any, don't give any. But no matter what you do, no posing. Don't appear to be one way when you're really something else. What a powerful lesson.

In the church, the presence of God was very strong, just as when Jesus was alive on the earth and all posers had to be uncovered immediately. A real church is not a place that coddles, pleases, respects and honors posers. A real church should be a place to make real posers uncomfortable, hopefully not dead, but uncomfortable.

We can no longer seek to coddle posers; we must tell the truth. The people of God must be real and authentic. This is the only way the Kingdom of God works. Warts? Welcome. Mistakes? Welcome. Posing? Dead.

The power of God was so strong during this time because Jesus had just left the earth. Comparatively speaking, the church operated with great power, but today it seems as if it is running only on fumes. I have a vision that the church can one day become as powerful as it was then but the first thing that must happen is to expose the posers.

We can no longer seek to coddle posers; we must tell the truth. The people of God must be real and authentic. This is the only way the Kingdom of God works. Warts? Welcome. Mistakes? Welcome. Posing? Dead. This is the way the first church was.

Another example takes place during Jesus's ministry. "Jesus sat down near the collection box in the temple and watched as the crowds dropped in their money."

What would you think at your church if, every Sunday, your pastor sat right next to the offering basket and watched what the people gave? Wouldn't that be odd?

My church would probably have zero people attending. They would be heard saying something like, "Do you know what the pastor did? He sat right down by the offering table and watched everyone put something in!"

When Jesus saw what everyone was giving, specifically the rich and their large amounts and the widow with her last two coins, He was looking at budgets, not amounts.

But Jesus Himself sat down near the collection box in the temple and watched as the crowds dropped in their money! What do you think He was doing there? He was exposing the posers. This was the life lesson that He was going to give to the disciples that day. "Many rich people put in large amounts—" See, this is why posers are allowed in the church today because pastors like large amounts.

"Many rich people put in large amounts. Then a poor widow came and dropped in two small coins" (Mark 12:41-42).

How did Jesus separate the authentic from the poser? Let's look again at those two verses. "Jesus sat down near the collection box in the temple and watched as the crowds dropped in their money. Many rich people put in large amounts. Then a poor widow came and dropped in two small coins."

Based on these two verses, wouldn't it be fair to say that Jesus looks at our budget to separate the authentic from the poser? When Jesus saw the amounts that everyone was giving, specifically the rich and their large amounts and the widow with her last two coins, He was looking at budgets, not amounts. Two coins was more than all the other large amounts put together. Why? Percentages. The percent indicates the authenticity.

Jesus says, "For where your treasure is, there will your heart be also" (Matthew 6:21).

The modern day church is all messed up. It's like having a mother who has issues, but you still love her.

Our youngest son works for a Christian organization as a web designer. From his very first check, he decided to give ten percent to our church. His older brother has done the exact same thing since high school. At the height of my business success, I was making $2,300.00 for a thirty-hour week and was having the time of my life. I would do a little work, make lots of money, and do things that were enjoyable for my family and me. Let's just say that I was giving $100 a week to the church.

Now, that sounds like a large amount. In fact, it's seven times more than what my son is giving right now at ten percent. Of course, the pastor is going to like me because I'm putting my hundred dollars in the offering basket. But in Jesus's world, I'm not giving enough according to what I make.

It seems the modern day church is all messed up. It's like having a mother who has issues, but you still love her. I love the church, even those who are posers. I love everyone just as Jesus loves everyone. He even loved Judas the same as He loved Peter.

At the Last Supper, no one knew who the betrayer was because Jesus didn't treat Judas any differently than He did the others. For three and a half years, He treated him and loved him exactly the same.

We're like the anti-Robin Hoods of modern society; we steal from the poor and keep it. But listen, we're only petty thieves. The organized church is grand theft auto.

The average Christian gives approximately three or four percent. Most Christians in America give less than that, a lot less. It's just like everything else: There are about twenty percent giving almost all of what comes in, which averages to three to four percent from each one.

The average person "claiming" to be a christian, steals six to seven percent from the poor, every week and then "claim" that God is pleased. We're like the anti-Robin Hoods of modern society; we steal from the poor and keep it. But listen, we're only petty thieves. The organized church is grand theft auto. They are in-your-face thieves.

Ninety eight percent of the church's budget, the tithe that is supposed to help the poor, is spent on the church. Only two percent goes to the poor and missions. According to God's accounting, seventy five percent should go to the poor; twenty five percent should go to the priest and none to the church. This is how we are to spend the ten percent.

If you want to build a church, that amount would be additional to the ten percent. The ten percent goes to the poor. There are no exceptions to that and anyone who keeps the tithe for any other purpose is called a "thief" in Malachi chapter three. Compared to the organized church, we are just petty thieves, because they're stealing 75% every week from the poor!

When I talk about the poor, I'm talking about those who are suffering this moment. In fact, 18,000 children die daily from starvation alone.

And guess what? We're celebrating it, like it's the greatest thing in the world, like we're the apple of God's eye. When I talk about the poor, I'm talking about those who are suffering this moment. In fact, 18,000 children die daily from starvation alone.

I'll give you two modern day examples:

Mega church 1: They receive $30,000.00 a week in offerings, a small amount for a mega church. And every week, they feed 100 homeless people. This costs approximately $300.00, and they celebrate their efforts like it's the greatest thing.

This is just one mega church! If that church gave 75% of their income to the poor, like they're supposed to, they could remove all homelessness in their city!

Mega church 2: This mega church has five different mega church campuses. Their budget is online and they receive twenty-four and a half million dollars every year! And every year, they give one and a half million to the poor. That's a lot of money!

Yet every year, they steal six and a half million dollars from the poor. We're never going to get anywhere unless we shine the light on the truth and accept the truth. Jesus looks at budgets and the first ten percent is to go to the poor, and if we're not doing that, we need to be honest about it.

Am I saying you can never have anything or do anything? No. God has richly blessed us for our enjoyment.

Am I saying you can never have anything or do anything? No. God has richly blessed us for our enjoyment. Allow me to share two of my own personal experiences:

Just recently, we received an IRS refund check. This was a miracle! I had no idea there was money coming, and the IRS contacted me and sent me a form to fill out, and when I received the check in the mail, my family and I were so excited, we felt like framing it!

Our younger son is saving up for his first car. So we began to think now is the time to purchase a second car and we figured we would sell our car to our son. As I began shopping for a vehicle, I came across a 2000 Jeep for $2,000.

Now, I could have taken that $2,000.00 and borrowed $8,000.00 to purchase a newer car. Just like Peter said to Ananias and Sapphira, "It's in your power to do". God would have allowed me to buy a $50,000.00 car if that's what I wanted to do.

But because this newly purchased car is paid off, I don't have any future expenses, which automatically frees me up to have more to help others who have nothing.

Right after purchasing our car, I received an email from Orbitz cruises. For $439.00, we could've gone on a wonderful 4-night cruise that would leave Miami, go to Key West and Cozumel, Mexico and back. We took our very first cruise a couple years earlier, also at a great price, and it was one of the best vacations we'd ever had.

We could have gone on that vacation if I wanted to. We did without something for the comfort of someone less fortunate.

So I did what I am going to teach you right now: "Blessed is he who considers the poor. The word "considers" means "to really give your attention to and then act accordingly". Helping the poor honors God.

A person who gets ahead by opposing the poor (by keeping from the poor what is rightfully theirs) or by showering gifts on the rich (just letting the posers get away with their posing) will end in poverty. Thus, consider the poor before you buy anything.

We could have gone on that vacation if I wanted to. Instead, we sent the money to fund the cost of digging a well for a village that is in need of clean water. We did without something for the comfort of someone less fortunate.

We did the same thing with our 1998 Suzuki. I chose to drive it instead of a Harley. I saved a ton of money, and it rides just like a Harley, and it's beautiful. I considered the poor.

Now, the second example: We live in Ponce Inlet, Florida in a very nice home, one block from the ocean. We've chosen to live in nice homes for our entire marriage. Because of this, we've cut down on all other expenses and try to live simply in all other areas.

Remember, Peter said, we're free to do whatever we want with what God gives is. All God asks is that we "consider" the poor. So, I urge you. Start today and consider the poor with every purchase you make.

One of my favorite Mother Teresa quotes: "Live simply so others may simply live."

CHAPTER FIVE

Fruit

In nature, we prune rose bushes, grapevines, fruit trees, and other bushes. The Wikipedia definition says you can reshape bushes and trees, while getting rid of the dead branches. You can even improve poor health of a tree or bush when you cut it back. If the plant is in good health, you can maintain its health by pruning it. There are so many benefits for one simple procedure.

The fruit gets picked for eating, but it's the branches that get pruned.

Let's say I'm the gardener and I have a vineyard. In my vineyard, I have a vine, a branch and fruit. What part of the plant gets pruned? The branch, right? We don't prune the vine and we don't prune the fruit. The fruit gets picked for eating, but it's the branches that get pruned.

Now, in Jesus's famous parable of a vineyard, there's a vineyard (which is the world), God's creation, and a gardener (who is God). And Jesus says in this vineyard, "I am the vine and you are the branch." Wait a minute, what part gets pruned again? I don't know about you, but I'm not sure that I like this idea. It doesn't sound so good to me.

> *When we get up in the morning, I'm sure most of us have not prayed, "God, please prune me today. Cut me back as far as you can."*

Now imagine a pair of clippers. Pruning is wonderful, unless you're the branch and you see those clippers coming at you! But remember, Jesus didn't ask us what we wanted. He didn't say, "What do you want to be when you grow up? Would you like to own a vineyard? Would you like to be the vine? Would you like to be the fruit? What would you like to be in my kingdom?"

Jesus said, "I am the vine and you are the branch." This goes against our nature. When we get up in the morning, I'm sure most of us have not prayed, "God, please prune me today. Cut me back as far as you can." It's just not in our nature.

Even though Hebrews 12:10-11 is referring to parenting, it can also be used in the context of pruning. "They disciplined us for a little while as they thought best; but God disciplines us for our good, in order that we may share in his holiness. No discipline seems pleasant at the time, but painful. Later on, however, it produces a harvest of righteousness and peace for those who have been trained by it."

As a father, when I correct my child, I am hoping to reshape his direction, cut off some dead weight, and improve his overall well-being. My ultimate hope is that he becomes a better person. That's what correction is for.

Anyone who does not remain in me is thrown away like a useless branch and withers.

Because we are branches, we have a choice to produce fruit. The vine can't produce fruit for you, nor can the gardener. No one can produce fruit for you. In John 15:6, Jesus says, "Anyone who does not remain in me is thrown away like a useless branch and withers. Such branches are gathered into a pile to be burned."

This verse should motivate you to be a branch that bears fruit. Let's take a look at verse 4, "Remain in me and I will remain in you for a branch cannot bear fruit if it is severed from the vine, you cannot be fruitful unless you remain in me. I am the vine, you are the branches. Those who remain in me and I in them will produce much fruit for apart from me you can do nothing."

Based on these two choices, there are three camps.

1) The Undecided

You can choose to be undecided about God until your last breath. But just keep in mind that 150,000 people die every day. Maybe you'll be one of them, maybe you won't. The risk is up to you.

2) The Fruitless Believer

This is a very popular camp in the church today. It's the camp that says, "I am a Christian, but I'm not producing fruit." Listen, God is not Bob Barker. There is no door number three, no third option. You're either producing fruit or you're not. According to the Word of God, if you're not producing fruit, you're thrown away and burned.

Jesus says that fruit is the only proof that you're a Christian.

Remember, it's your choice, but if you choose to not produce fruit you will be cut off, thrown away and burned. Somehow, today, we've redefined what grace means, which is to never produce fruit, yet believe we're fine.

If you believe this way, I hope you're right. But I don't see it. As far as I can tell, Jesus says that fruit is the only proof that you're a Christian. But bearing fruit is not just saying that you're a Christian. If you're not bearing fruit, you're better off in the first camp. In contrast, it's a very scary thing to say, "I know I'm saved, but I don't have any fruit. But I'm fine with that. Everything is all good."

3) The Fruit-Producing Christian

This is the camp to be in. But remember, you can't bear fruit without being pruned. If you're still reading this book, it's a good sign that you want to produce fruit in your life and you are willing to be pruned along the way.

To help you get started, answer the following question.

"How do I bear fruit?"

John 15:4-5 says, "Abide in me, and I in you. As the branch cannot bear fruit of itself, except it abide in the vine; no more can ye, except ye abide in me. I am the vine, ye are the branches: He that abideth in me, and I in him, the same bringeth forth much fruit: for without me ye can do nothing."

According to Webster's Dictionary, the word "abide" means to "wait for or to accept without objection." Objection means "feeling or expressing disapproval or dissent." Well, that's a nice definition, but there's a problem: That is the exact opposite of human nature!

As a human being, my nature is to force something to happen, fret about it, and if nothing else works, just freak out completely. These reactions come naturally to us.

The scriptures say that the Roman government was a disaster, yet Jesus walked this earth "abiding" in His Father. For us to walk in the same way, we must do two secrets. The reason I call them secrets is because they are hidden in plain view in the parable of the vine.

The Vineyard

The first secret is that the vineyard, although really messed up, is not ours to fix. In this analogy, Jesus is trying to teach us our role as a branch. If we want to learn to abide, we must understand that it's His vineyard to rule, not ours. Our job is to learn to abide and wait without objection, and not express disapproval and dissent.

> *I cannot take care of His vineyard. That's His job, I'm a branch and my responsibility is to live without expressing any disapproval on how God cares for His vineyard.*

If that's our job, then why do we spend half our lives trying to fix things in His vineyard? I know that if we were in charge of the vineyard, we'd do things a lot differently. We would eradicate all evil.

But the gardener seems to think His way is better. If we were ever to get our own vineyard, we could run it our way, but right now, we're in His vineyard, playing by His rules.

Honestly, sometimes when I wake up, the weight of this vineyard is heavy, and my very first thought is, *I need to fix this vineyard today! If I don't fix it soon, it'll get worse!* But whenever I have those thoughts, I do my best to say, "Hey, God! Your vineyard is really messed up. You have some work to do today!"

Because it's His vineyard, can we trust him? I cannot take care of His vineyard. That's His job, I'm a branch and my responsibility is to live without expressing any disapproval on how God cares for His vineyard.

Jesus is the Vine

The second secret is Jesus is the vine. The vine is one hundred percent responsible for all juice. The branch produces no juice, no strength, no life whatsoever. You understand that you have not produced or created your own breath. We are allowed to be here. Jesus says, "Apart from me you can do nothing."

> *Whatever issues are going on in the vineyard, Jesus says, "I am the vine and I will supply anything and everything you need. No matter what comes, I'm in control."*

When you understand that Jesus is the vine, it helps you to abide. The God of the universe is one hundred percent responsible for your health, your well-being, and your daily bread.

Even so, half of me tries to fix the vineyard and the other half of me tries to get more juice. Some mornings, my prayers sound like Captain Kirk, "Scotty! I need more juice!" Whatever issues are going on in the vineyard, Jesus says, "I am the vine and I will supply anything and everything you need. No matter what comes, I'm in control."

Philippians 4:19 says, "And this same God who takes care of me will supply all your need from his glorious riches which have been given to us in Christ Jesus."

2 Corinthians 9:8 says, "And God will generously provide all you need, then you will always have everything you need and plenty left over to share with others."

Whatever amount of juice we have today, that's our daily bread. And we need to have peace about that.

Romans 8:28 says, "We know that God causes everything to work together for the good for those who love God and are called according to His purpose." Even in this crazy, mixed-up vineyard, we trust Him to figure it all out.

Verse 41 says, "If God is for us, who can ever be against us? Since he did not spare his own Son but gave him up for us all, won't he also give us everything we need?"

But if we spend every waking hour saying, "I need more juice", it's the exact opposite of abiding. Whatever amount of juice we have today, that's our daily bread. And we need to have peace about that. Who does He work everything out for; branches that abide.

If we abide in Him and His word abides in us, we will bear much fruit. In the next chapter, we will define exactly what this fruit is according to John the Baptist and Jesus own teachings.

CHAPTER SIX

Carded

If you've ever been pulled over by a police officer, the first thing they ask for is your ID. The same goes with going through checkpoints, security, or entering a new country. Even at Sam's Club, there is usually someone standing at the door, who will only allow you into the store when you show them your Sam's card.

When you get pulled over and you have no proof that you can legally drive, what happens? No more driving for you.

In any of these scenarios, why are they asking for your ID? It's because they want proof that you are who you claim to be.

What happens if you're in a situation where your identification is required and you have no proof? When you get pulled over and you have no proof that you can legally drive, what happens? No more driving for you. If you show up at customs and you have no passport or ID, what happens? They will not allow you to enter.

Even if we offer some great argument, how effective are we going to be at TSA if we try to talk our way through without a ticket or identification?

The scriptures tell us repeatedly that Judgment Day is a day of showing ID.

The more important the access, the less likely it would be for you to get in without the proper ID. You may be able to get past the Sam's Club person, but when it came time to check out, you would not be able to purchase anything without your card.

There are times when certain establishments go a little overboard, but generally speaking, it's a good thing. I think it's great that minors can't purchase controlled substances. I also think it's great that wanted criminals or terrorists cannot board airplanes. I think it's smart for officials to want to know who is entering their country. That's just common sense.

Let's say someone is endeavoring to leave the country, and they know they are going through TSA and customs. What would we call a person who doesn't bring their proof? At best, they are misinformed and are making some grave mistake.

I don't know about you, but when I travel, I check fifteen times before leaving the house to make sure I have my ticket and all forms of identification.

The scriptures tell us repeatedly that Judgment Day is a day of showing ID. It is a day of proving who you are.

Jesus himself said that it's very foolish to live this life without preparing for that day. If you want to pass from this world into His kingdom, you must have proof that you are His child.

The Bible says it's only by grace that you are saved, but you must prove your faith. You can go to the checkpoint and say anything, but if you want entrance, you must have proof.

When I turned 18, I went to a bar. I was doing something I should not have been doing, and a huge bouncer grabbed me from behind, took me outside, threw me on the ground, and said, "Don't you ever come back here!" I had just been bounced! Well, I don't want to get bounced that day when entering heaven.

How do we prove to God that we are His? John 15:8 says, "When you produce much fruit, you are my true disciples. This brings great glory to my Father." If you have no fruit in your life, don't expect to show up at heaven's gates, thinking God will slide you in.

Without fruit, we get bounced. The Bible says it's only by grace that you are saved, but you must prove your faith. You can go to the checkpoint and say anything, but if you want entrance, you must have proof.

Luke 3:8-9 says, "Prove by the way you live that you have repented of your sins and turned to God."

Revelation 2:23 says, "All the churches shall know that I am he that searches minds and hearts and I will give unto every one of you according to your actions."

Romans 2:6 says, "He will judge everyone according to what they have done."

We need to think about what we are planning to offer God when we meet Him. Many of us are going to get to the security checkpoint and say, "I'm a citizen. You know I am! I told everyone I really like that country. I even put it on my Facebook status!"

Don't bring God fruit that you think He wants. Bring God the fruit that He commands.

And according to Matthew 25:31-46, Jesus will say, "Where's your ID? Where's your proof that you are who you say you are?" And many will respond, "Jesus died for me. His blood cleansed me". But those are just words. Jesus is asking us for *proof* that we are His followers.

I'm sure you've heard the story of Cain and Abel. Abel offered God an animal sacrifice and Cain offered the fruit of his labor, but it was not what God asked for. It wasn't that Cain's offering was evil, it simply was not what God wanted. So, God rejected Cain's offering. He was "bounced". Then he became very angry and murdered Abel out of jealous rage.

Don't bring God fruit that you *think* He wants. Bring God the fruit that He commands. When I was 19, I stopped smoking, drinking, getting high and cussing overnight. I just woke up one morning and I changed my actions. That's not fruit. Anyone can do that. Don't get me wrong. It's good, and I can offer it to God, but it's not fruit. It's a Cain offering.

The Final Judgment

So what does Jesus want? Matthew 25:31-34 says, "But when the Son of Man comes in his glory, and all the angels with him, then he will sit upon his glorious throne. All the nations will be gathered in his presence, and he will separate the people as a shepherd separates the sheep from the goats. He will place the sheep at his right hand and the goats at his left.

> *Words don't prove anything. Good actions don't prove anything. God wants a specific offering.*

"Then the King will say to those on his right, 'Come, you who are blessed by my Father, inherit the Kingdom prepared for you from the creation of the world."

Why were those people granted access into God's kingdom? Words don't prove anything. Good actions don't prove anything. God wants a specific offering and it's found in the following verses:

Matthew 25:35-44 says, "For I was hungry, and you fed me. I was thirsty, and you gave me a drink. I was a stranger, and you invited me into your home. I was naked, and you gave me clothing. I was sick, and you cared for me. I was in prison, and you visited me.'

"Then these righteous ones will reply, 'Lord, when did we ever see you hungry and feed you? Or thirsty and give you something to drink? Or a stranger and show you hospitality? Or naked and give you clothing? When did we ever see you sick or in prison and visit you?'

Away with you, you cursed ones, into the eternal fire prepared for the devil and his demons. For I was hungry, and you didn't feed me.

"And the King will say, 'I tell you the truth, when you did it to one of the least of these my brothers and sisters, you were doing it to me!'

"Then the King will turn to those on the left and say, 'Away with you, you cursed ones, into the eternal fire prepared for the devil and his demons. For I was hungry, and you didn't feed me. I was thirsty, and you didn't give me a drink. I was a stranger, and you didn't invite me into your home. I was naked, and you didn't give me clothing. I was sick and in prison, and you didn't visit me.'

"Then they will reply, 'Lord, when did we ever see you hungry or thirsty or a stranger or naked or sick or in prison, and not help you?'"

This is it! These verses outline the kind of fruit Jesus is looking for. I tell my church, "If you're unwilling to give this kind of fruit, please keep coming so I can change your mind. Because it's the proof you need to enter God's kingdom!"

So often, we substitute a good offering for the *specific* offering that God wants. God wants us to help the least of these. Who are the least? The poor, the destitute, the oppressed, the humiliated, the defenseless, the needy, the weak, the dependent, the socially inferior. John the Baptist agreed with Jesus in Luke 3:10: "The crowds asked, 'What should we do?' John replied, 'If you have two shirts give one to the poor, if you have food share it with those who are hungry.'"

Helping someone who cannot return the favor is a beautiful picture of what Christ did for us when He died on the cross and paid for our sins.

You must prepare to meet God! Arrange your life so that the poor come first. Pharisees will do anything for God, except put the poor first. Sadly, I've discovered that the modern church is like the Pharisees in this way. They have decided to bring God something else.

Why is God requiring us to put the poor before everything else? Because helping the poor is a pure, selfless act. There's no return. There's no benefit. Helping someone who cannot return the favor is a beautiful picture of what Christ did for us when He died on the cross and paid for our sins.

There's no other benefit when you help the poor, except bringing glory to God. If you're helping the poor to be seen by others, 1 Corinthians 13 says it means nothing. For your fruit to glorify God, you must help the poor with no ulterior motives.

And it just so happens that helping the poor is a great way to practice being selfless. Our hearts need some type of healing, a cleansing from self-absorption and self-indulgence. It's not that caring for yourself is evil. But as you mature in God, you will become less selfish, and it will be more natural to think of the poor first.

Apprentices don't work on the outside first. They work on the inside first. You get the inside clean by committing selfless acts.

When we care for the poor, it allows us to act selflessly without getting anything in return. If I love my wife, Nina, I get an immediate reward.

Maybe you're thinking, *I'm going to love my friends, family, and neighbors, and I'm not going to do any harm to anyone, and I'm just going to be kind to everyone. I'm going to offer God that.* But that is not enough.

Matthew 23:25 says, "Woe to you, teachers of the law and Pharisees, you hypocrites! You clean the outside of the cup and dish, but inside they are full of greed and self-indulgence."

Jesus is saying you have to get to the inside. Apprentices don't work on the outside first. They work on the inside first. You get the inside clean by committing selfless acts. What a great way to live!

Jesus said in Luke 11:41, "so clean the inside by giving gifts to the poor and you will be clean all over."

CHAPTER SEVEN

Random Acts of Kindness

Mark Twain once said, "Kindness is a language that the deaf can hear and the blind can see." Kindness is really important and the Bible teaches how important it is.

There is evil in this world and the evil will defeat the good if there is no course of action to follow.

I'm sure you've heard the phrase "random acts of kindness". Although I love the kindness part, I don't like the "random" part so much. Webster's Dictionary defines random as a "haphazard course without definite aim, direction or method." I don't think this is how God wants us to treat kindness. There is evil in this world and the evil will defeat the good if there is no course of action to follow.

There are a lot of things that need more than "random". You wouldn't say, "I perform random acts of gardening", would you? What would a garden look like if the gardener cared for it randomly? Not much, right? The weeds, bugs and animals would destroy it.

Try to get your acts of kindness out of the *random* world and into the *priority* world. Let me give you an example of what my priorities are in an average workday:

I usually go for a bike ride when I first wake up around 7:00. When I get back home around 7:30, I do some morning grooming. Then I have two main priorities. First, I drink a glass of cold water, and secondly, I drink a decaf iced coffee. Then I go to work. In the summer, I work until about 11:30, and then I come home to eat lunch.

> *When I stand before my congregation, I don't say what I want to say. I spend much of my workday thinking and preparing what God wants me to say.*

Notice my priorities? Coffee and lunch, two very important things in my day. Then I continue with my work until about mid-afternoon. Then around 3:15, I have a snack, which almost always consists of 85% dark chocolate, and then I'm ready to finish my work.

When my work is finished, we have dinner. Once dinner is over, I have a little "me time", because when you spend hours a day saving the world …haha… with prayer, study, and sermon preparation, etc., your mind can turn to mush. My "me time" consists of watching some TV, my favorite shows, sports, or movies. This time helps me to unwind and relax my mind because I do a lot of thinking.

I take my job seriously. When I stand before our congregation, I don't say what I want to say. I spend much of my workday thinking and preparing what God wants me to say. A person who speaks for God should take it very seriously. And I do.

According to the scriptures, you can't put Jesus first until you put the "least" first.

When God led me into the ministry, He revealed Acts 6, where Peter, James and John say, "We will give ourselves continually to prayer and the ministry of the Word." And I felt the Spirit of God say, "That's what I want you to do for a living!"

In the beginning, it was tough! It was like pulling teeth. Today, it's one of the easier things I do. I pray, meditate, seek God, write notes, study, and research. I've put in tens of thousands of hours over the years, and it's now one of the easiest things I do.

That's what I do for a living. God said, "If you'll do that for a living, I will take care of you." He has proven faithful to His word.

When I say put "kindness" at the top of your priority list, I'm not saying to throw out work, family, relationships, food or coffee! On the contrary, the Bible says to enjoy all good things. But those who want to follow Jesus must also make kindness a part of their priority list.

Until you make this a priority, you're not really following Jesus. According to the scriptures, you can't put Jesus first until you put the "least" first. This is where our acts of kindness come in.

Why do you think it's so hard to be kind to those less fortunate? Jesus said the root issue is greed, self-indulgence, and self-interest. And as far as I can see from studying the scriptures, the one thing that attacks a greedy and selfish heart is selfless acts of kindness. Clean the inside of the cup by giving gifts to the poor.

Every single time you are kind to someone, your greedy and self-indulgent heart will be cleansed.

I can support this claim with eighty different passages in the Bible. You can go to our webpage at www.poncechurch.com and click on the section titled: "80 Bible Passages on Social Justice". Not verses, *passages*. Or simply, skip over to chapter nine of this book.

The heart of man is greedy and self-indulgent, and it can only be clean by selfless acts of kindness, and the only way to ensure that it's a selfless act is to serve those who can never repay you.

Let's be real. Your individual acts of kindness will not cure the world. Sadly, most people need more than just one person to help them. As I have been writing this book, I've been helping a homeless man who's as stubborn as they come.

If you've ever tried to give homeless people ideas to improve their situation, they'll usually list ten reasons why it won't work. In this particular man's case, he refuses to change.

As you pursue kindness, don't become discouraged. You can't save the world. No one can. Many times, you will not see any change in the person you're helping. That's just the way it is, but every single time you are kind to someone, your greedy and self-indulgent heart will be cleansed. Even a cup of cold water attacks selfishness at the root.

> *All He's asking of us is to add kindness to our lives in a planned way.*

Ephesians 5:5 says, "You can be sure that no immoral, impure or greedy person will inherit the kingdom of Christ and of God, for a greedy person is an idolater worshiping the things of this world."

It's human nature to be consumers, but that doesn't make it any less sinful. All we want is more. Think about Adam and Eve in the Garden of Eden. They had everything the heart could ever want, including God Himself. It wasn't enough. They had to have that one thing they didn't have. We're constantly telling ourselves we need more of this and more of that. We need this person to change or this situation to be different.

How does one get rid of our consumerism nature? Luke 11:41 says, "Clean the inside by giving gifts to the poor." That's how we do it.

Ephesians 5:1-2 says, "Imitate God, therefore, in everything you do, for you are his dear children. Live a life filled with love, following the example of Christ. He loved us and offered himself as a sacrifice for us, a pleasing aroma to God." Remember, we are to imitate God as dear children. How? By selflessly giving up our lives for others.

God's not saying to never enjoy anything in life, never have work, never have friends, never have 'me' time, never have an iced coffee, never have snacks and food, and so on. All He's asking of us is to add kindness to our lives in a planned way. Remember, it should not be random acts of kindness. It should be thought out ahead of time.

Jesus lived His whole life doing selfless acts and being kind to people. To be like Jesus, that's what we must do, too.

1 John 4:7-11 says, "Dear friends, let us continue to love one another for love comes from God. Anyone who loves is a child of God and knows God. But anyone who does not love does not know God, for God is love. God showed how much he loved us by sending his one and only Son into the world so that we might have eternal life through him. This is real love—not that we loved God, but that He loved us and sent His Son as a sacrifice to take away our sins. Dear friends, since God loved us that much, we surely ought to love each other."

If we're going to be apprentices of Jesus, we need to practice this love on purpose.

Acts 10:38 says, "You know that God anointed Jesus of Nazareth with the Holy Spirit and with power, then Jesus went about doing good and healing all that were oppressed by the devil, for God was with him."

Jesus lived His whole life doing selfless acts and being kind to people. To be like Jesus, that's what we must do, too.

Here are a few ideas to get you started

I encourage you to plan an act/event of kindness once a month. Put it on your calendar and plan it. It may be visiting a widow in your neighborhood. It can also be the poor, the sick, the hurting, or those who are in prison.

It needs to include anyone whom Jesus calls the "least". It can even be the person no one else wants to be around. You might say, "Is that what it means to be like Jesus?" Yes! That's what it means to imitate God and be like Jesus.

Once you pick someone, decide what you'll do. It can be something as simple as a dinner at your home. Or volunteer somewhere, such as feeding the homeless or visiting the sick. Whatever it is, you have to plan it or you'll never do it.

Then, when you're comfortable with once a month, you can begin to plan for twice a month. What are you waiting for? Start planning today!

CHAPTER EIGHT

The Main Thing

Steven Covey, a businessman and author who sold over twenty five million copies, famously said, "The main thing, is to keep the main thing, the main thing." When it comes to Christianity, is there a main thing? And if so, what is it?

Basically, we're all set on ninety five percent of what we know and believe.

There are two things that modern science has told us. One is that everyone is only willing to change about five percent of what they currently believe. Basically, we're all set on ninety five percent of what we know and believe, and that ninety five percent of what we know and believe, we've decided that we are sure we're right.

The second thing that modern science has told us is that every second of our life, our brain is receiving four hundred billion bits of information. That is equivalent to six hundred thousand books of information! Now, no one can handle that. Maybe once we get to heaven, we'll be able to process all four hundred billion bits of information.

Our brain has the capacity to filter out everything but two thousand bits per second. We have to admit that's quite a bit of information. We're looking at color, sounds, smells, light and more without even really knowing it. Our brain taps into all of it.

We're so sure as individuals, yet we're missing almost everything. We can only filter in so much.

So that we don't go insane, our brain only processes two thousand bits of information versus four hundred billion bits. But here's the thing, if we're filtering out over three hundred and ninety nine billion bits of information every second, how do we know we're not filtering out the wrong stuff? Your odds aren't very good. We're talking about one half of one millionth of a percent is what we call reality. That's all that's registering.

What if we're receiving the wrong two thousand bits? How many of you agree with me that Jesus received a different two thousand bits than everyone else? He chose to get a different two thousand bits. He was way out there.

All I'm saying is, we're so sure as individuals, yet we're missing almost everything. We can only filter in so much and all of that comes from our childhood, our training, all of these different factors we're filtering, filtering, filtering down.

It's possible that newborn babies are getting it all. If you look at a newborn baby, you can tell that they're processing a lot of information just by their expressions and if you watch how they look around, they have a look like, "Whoa, what's going on?" They're possibly receiving it all, but as we get older, we learn to filter it down.

Since we have so many experts making all kinds of claims, what is the main thing?

But when a baby is born, it has inside itself the ability to speak any language and make any sound, but their brain filters all of that out to the language they hear. But if you take that same baby to another country and it grows up in that culture, it will learn to speak that language perfectly because it has the capacity to.

It's so easy for us to be convinced in our own minds, without even knowing about the three hundred and ninety nine billion bits that are floating around.

It happens in groups as well. The more people agree with you about a subject, the more certain you become about it. When that happens, it becomes almost impenetrable.

Let me ask you a question. Since we have so many experts making all kinds of claims, what *is* the main thing? Sadly, if you go into three hundred and thirty thousand churches today, you might hear three hundred and thirty thousand different main things. Now, let me ask you this, who is the most qualified person to ask what the main thing is? God and Jesus, right? Well (and I say this humorously), if only there was a book or a source with His words written down that we could consult on the issue. Ah! There is one!

> *If you have two shirts, give one to the poor. If you have food, share it with those who are hungry.*

Let's see what Jesus Himself says to the religious leaders. Matthew 21:32 says, "For John the Baptist came and showed you the right way to live, but you didn't believe him, while tax collectors and prostitutes did."

Isn't that interesting? Religious experts didn't believe when common people did. Notice, Jesus and John the Baptist have a main thing that's different from everyone else.

Let's take a look at what Jesus and John the Baptist say about the "main" thing. Luke 3:9-10 says, "Even now the ax of God's judgment is poised, ready to sever the roots of the trees. Yes, every tree that does not produce good fruit will be chopped down and thrown into the fire. The crowds asked, 'What should we do?' John replied, 'If you have two shirts, give one to the poor. If you have food, share it with those who are hungry.'"

According to John the Baptist, the "main" thing involves taking on the yoke of Jesus, easing another's burden, and lightening another's load. Jesus said that John came to show us the way to live and we rejected it.

If you want to know what Jesus Himself believes is the main thing, read Matthew 25:31-34, which says, "But when the Son of Man comes in his glory, and all the angels with him, then he will sit upon his glorious throne. All the nations will be gathered in his presence, and he will separate the people as a shepherd separates the sheep from the goats. He will place the sheep at his right hand and the goats at his left. And the King will say…"

Come, you who are blessed by my Father; take your inheritance, the kingdom prepared for you since the creation of the world.

Let's stop here for a moment. Can you agree that Jesus is getting ready to say something important? He says, "All nations will be gathered." That means every human being will be in His presence. Wouldn't that be a great time to tell us what the main thing is?

Matthew 25:34-46 says, "Then the King will say to those on his right, 'Come, you who are blessed by my Father; take your inheritance, the kingdom prepared for you since the creation of the world. For I was hungry and you gave me something to eat, I was thirsty and you gave me something to drink, I was a stranger and you invited me in, I needed clothes and you clothed me, I was sick and you looked after me, I was in prison and you came to visit me.'

"Then the righteous will answer him, 'Lord, when did we see you hungry and feed you, or thirsty and give you something to drink? When did we see you a stranger and invite you in, or needing clothes and clothe you? When did we see you sick or in prison and go to visit you?'

The number one thing on God's mind is the fact that humans are suffering in this world.

"The King will reply, 'Truly I tell you, whatever you did for one of the least of these brothers and sisters of mine, you did for me.'

"Then he will say to those on his left, 'Depart from me, you who are cursed, into the eternal fire prepared for the devil and his angels. For I was hungry and you gave me nothing to eat, I was thirsty and you gave me nothing to drink, I was a stranger and you did not invite me in, I needed clothes and you did not clothe me, I was sick and in prison and you did not look after me.'

"They also will answer, 'Lord, when did we see you hungry or thirsty or a stranger or needing clothes or sick or in prison, and did not help you?'

"He will reply, 'Truly I tell you, whatever you did not do for one of the least of these, you did not do for me.'

"Then they will go away to eternal punishment, but the righteous to eternal life."

It's very simple. According to Jesus, helping the "least" is the main thing. The number one thing on God's mind is the fact that humans are suffering in this world. Now, many of us spend our time trying to hide from it, and I understand that. But God's main concern is human suffering.

When Jesus came here, His main thing was not building some kind of government or some type of political position. He did not try to form some kind of power structure. His main thing was not even condemning sinners. In fact, the tax collectors and prostitutes loved His message. He didn't even spend time trying to fix religion because He knew it was hopeless. The religious leaders of His time thought He was a nut. Why?

From the time Jesus woke up to the time He went to sleep, He spent His days healing, comforting, restoring, setting free, and delivering humanity from their suffering. That was His main thing.

From the time Jesus woke up to the time He went to sleep, He spent His days healing, comforting, restoring, setting free, and delivering humanity from their suffering. That was His main thing.

Isn't that true of a good father? If you had a suffering child, wouldn't everything else be secondary? For example, you may have heard about the young Marine who recently spent time in a Mexican jail. During his time of incarceration, his mother's main thing was to get her son released. That was all she thought about. That's what a good parent does. God is a good parent and the only thing on His mind is the hurting. Everything else is secondary.

As believers, it's our job to mirror Christ. Somehow, some way, we must stop the suffering. Jesus says that even a cup of cold water will stop the suffering of a person who is thirsty.

If you're in an emergency room and someone has constant bleeding because of an injury, what is the main thing? Stop the bleeding. The trauma team doesn't stand around saying, "How did that happen? We need to discuss this." No, there's only one thing on their mind and that is to stop the bleeding.

> *The world rejects Jesus' main thing through selfishness. Religion rejects Jesus' main thing through exalting minor things above the main thing.*

In the space of eternity, we are just a small little blip of a six thousand year span where there is suffering, and all God can think about during this little blip is to ease and comfort that suffering. Religion always rejects God's main thing—always has, probably always will.

It drove religious people nuts when Jesus would heal on the Sabbath or walk through the grains and pick when He was hungry. Why? Because He was violating their main thing, even when He told them that those things were secondary.

The world rejects Jesus' main thing through selfishness. Religion rejects Jesus' main thing through exalting minor things above the main thing. It puts anything else—worship, personal devotions, evangelism, fellowship, learning, serving—above the main thing and that's when those things become religion.

Matthew 21:42 says, "Didn't you read this in scripture that the stone that the builders rejected has now become the cornerstone."

I have read the whole Bible a number of times, and after a while, you can feel weighted down by all that's inside. Why? Because no one can do it all.

In ancient times, the cornerstone was the most important stone in a building. In pictures, you'll see this large stone that was set in the corner of where you wanted to build, and once that stone was set, you knew where to put every other stone or brick. All you had to do was line it up with that cornerstone in either direction, and all the smaller stones knew exactly where to go.

But Jesus said the "builders" rejected the cornerstone. This is very similar to when He was weeping over Jerusalem because they had rejected His teaching.

Notice, He didn't say that the world rejected this stone. The builders of God's house rejected this stone. We reject the stone when we exalt other stones above the cornerstone.

How many of you know the Bible is a big book? I have read the whole Bible a number of times, and after a while, you can feel weighted down by all that's inside. Why? Because no one can do it all. Not now, not ever. Still, religion puts pressure on us to do so. Did you know that only 17.7% of the American church attends regularly?

In previous years, it was 40%, but recent discoveries have shown that there are approximately eighty million people who say they attend regularly, but don't. It's a huge phenomenon.

Basically, Jesus said that we're omitting the weightier matters (the more important things) because we're so burdened down with the minor things.

I think the reason is, people are just burdened down. There are too many "minor" things being added as the "main" thing.

Basically, Jesus said that we're omitting the weightier matters (the more important things) because we're so burdened down with the minor things. But in reality, all that matters is that you keep the main thing the main thing.

Life is an emergency room, and we have a crucial task to do: relieve suffering. The other stuff is nice, like icing on a cake, but it's not the main thing.

In conclusion, "As he came close to Jerusalem, he saw the city ahead and he began to weep, 'How I wish today that you of all people would understand the way of peace but now it's too late and peace is hidden from your eyes" (Luke 19:41-42).

You may be wondering how long God has cared for the least. Well, I've been studying this very subject for fourteen years now, and I just saw this verse as I was writing this book.

Exodus 23:10 says, "Plant and harvest your crops for six years but let the land be renewed and lie uncultivated during the seventh year. Let the poor among you harvest whatever grows on it and leave the rest for the wild animals to eat and the same applies to your vineyards and olive groves."

> *God told the Israelites, "I'm going to remind you how important the poor are to me." He also said, "Every seven years, you're going to forgive all their debt."*

I consider myself an expert on this subject, yet that verse blew me away! Can you imagine being an Israelite back then?

People must've asked them, "Why aren't you working?"

"Oh, I'm letting the land rest."

"Why are you letting the land rest?"

"So the poor can have it."

God told the Israelites, "I'm going to remind you how important the poor are to me." He also said, "Every seven years, you're going to forgive all their debt."

Can you imagine meeting Jesus one day and hearing Him say, "What in the world were you thinking? I didn't mean for you to literally ease human suffering. I didn't mean all those words I said. All of those descriptions of me doing that in the Bible were all misconstrued. Those were just spiritual analogies. I didn't mean for you to actually do it. What were you thinking to actually comfort someone? What's wrong with you?"

That makes no sense! But I can imagine Him saying, "Why were you putting minor things above the main thing?" And so, as you continue along your Christian journey, remember to keep the main thing, the main thing.

CHAPTER NINE

213 Bible Verses on Our Response to Poverty (KJV)

- ***De 12:19***—*Take heed to thyself that thou forsake not the Levite as long as thou livest upon the earth.*

- ***De 14:28***—*At the end of three years thou shalt bring forth all the tithe of thine increase the same year, and shalt lay [it] up within thy gates:*

- ***De 14:29***—*And the Levite, (because he hath no part nor inheritance with thee,) and the stranger, and the fatherless, and the widow, which [are] within thy gates, shall come, and shall eat and be satisfied; that the LORD thy God may bless thee in all the work of thine hand which thou doest.*

- **De 15:7**—*If there be among you a poor man of one of thy brethren within any of thy gates in thy land which the LORD thy God giveth thee, thou shalt not harden thine heart, nor shut thine hand from thy poor brother:*

- **De 15:8**—*But thou shalt open thine hand wide unto him, and shalt surely lend him sufficient for his need, [in that] which he wanteth.*

- **De 15:10**—*Thou shalt surely give him, and thine heart shall not be grieved when thou givest unto him: because that for this thing the LORD thy God shall bless thee in all thy works, and in all that thou puttest thine hand unto.*

- **De 15:11**—*For the poor shall never cease out of the land: therefore I command thee, saying, Thou shalt open thine hand wide unto thy brother, to thy poor, and to thy needy, in thy land.*

- **De 24:14**—*Thou shalt not oppress an hired servant [that is] poor and needy, [whether he be] of thy brethren, or of thy strangers that [are] in thy land within thy gates: 17 Thou shalt not pervert the judgment of the stranger, nor of the fatherless; nor take a widow's raiment to pledge: 18 But thou shalt remember that thou wast a bondman in Egypt, and the LORD thy God redeemed thee thence: therefore I command thee to do this thing. 19 When thou cuttest down thine* *harvest in thy field, and hast forgot a sheaf in the field, thou shalt not go again to fetch it: it shall be for the stranger, for the fatherless, and for the widow: that the LORD thy God may bless thee in all the work of thine hands. 20 When thou beatest thine olive tree, thou shalt not go over the boughs again: it shall be for the stranger, for the fatherless, and for the widow. 21 When thou gatherest the grapes of thy vineyard, thou shalt not glean it afterward: it shall be for the stranger, for the fatherless, and for the widow. 22 And thou shalt remember that thou wast a bondman in the land of Egypt: therefore I command thee to do this thing.*

- *De 26:12—When thou hast made an end of tithing all the tithes of thine increase the third year, which is the year of tithing, and hast given it unto the Levite, the stranger, the fatherless, and the widow, that they may eat within thy gates, and be filled; 13 Then thou shalt say before the LORD thy God, I have brought away the hallowed things out of mine house, and also have given them unto the Levite, and unto the stranger, to the fatherless, and to the widow, according to all thy commandments which thou hast commanded me: I have not transgressed thy commandments, neither have I forgotten them:*

- *De 26:18—And the LORD hath avouched thee this day to be his peculiar people, as he hath promised thee, and that [thou] shouldest keep all his commandments;*

- *De 26:19—And to make thee high above all nations which he hath made, in praise, and in name, and in honour; and that thou mayest be an holy people unto the LORD thy God, as he hath spoken.*

- *Es 9:22—As the days wherein the Jews rested from their enemies, and the month which was turned unto them from sorrow to joy, and from mourning into a good day: that they should make them days of feasting and joy, and of sending portions one to another, and gifts to the poor.*

- *Job 20:10—His children shall seek to please the poor, and his hands shall restore their goods. 19 Because he hath oppressed and hath forsaken the poor; because he hath violently taken away an house which he builded not; 20 Surely he shall not feel quietness in his belly, he shall not save of that which he desired.*

- *Job 24:1—Why, seeing times are not hidden from the Almighty, do they that know him not see his days? 2 Some remove the landmarks; they violently take away flocks, and feed thereof. 3 They drive away the ass of the fatherless, they take the widow's ox for a pledge. 4 They turn the needy out of the way: the poor of the earth hide themselves together.*

- *Job 29:12— Because I delivered the poor that cried, and the fatherless, and him that had none to help him. 13 The blessing of him that was ready to perish came upon me: and I caused the widow's heart to sing for joy. 14 I put on righteousness, and it clothed me: my judgment was as a robe and a diadem. 15 I was eyes to the blind, and feet was I to the lame. 16 I was a father to the poor: and the cause which I knew not I searched out. 17 And I brake the jaws of the wicked, and plucked the spoil out of his teeth.*

- *Job 31:16—If I have withheld the poor from their desire, or have caused the eyes of the widow to fail; 17 Or have eaten my morsel myself alone, and the fatherless hath not eaten thereof; 19 If I have seen any perish for want of clothing, or any poor without covering; 21 If I have lifted up my hand against the fatherless, when I saw my help in the gate: 22 Then let mine arm fall from my shoulder blade, and mine arm be broken from the bone.*

- *Ps 12:5—For the oppression of the poor, for the sighing of the needy, now will I arise, saith the LORD; I will set [him] in safety [from him that] puffeth at him.*

- **Ps 37:21**—*The wicked borroweth, and payeth not again: but the righteous sheweth mercy, and giveth.*

- **Ps 41:1**—*Blessed is he that considereth the poor: the LORD will deliver him in time of trouble. 2 The LORD will preserve him, and keep him alive; and he shall be blessed upon the earth: and thou wilt not deliver him unto the will of his enemies.*

- **Ps 82:2**—*How long will ye judge unjustly, and accept the persons of the wicked? Selah. 3 Defend the poor and fatherless: do justice to the afflicted and needy. 4 Deliver the poor and needy: rid them out of the hand of the wicked.*

- **Ps 109:16**—*Because that he remembered not to shew mercy, but persecuted the poor and needy man, that he might even slay the broken in heart. 17 As he loved cursing, so let it come unto him: as he delighted not in blessing, so let it be far from him.*

- **Ps 112:1**—*Praise ye the LORD. Blessed [is] the man [that] feareth the LORD, [that] delighteth greatly in his commandments.*

- **Ps 112:3**—*Wealth and riches [shall be] in his house: and his righteousness endureth forever.*

- *Ps 112:9*—He hath dispersed, he hath given to the poor; his righteousness endureth forever; his horn shall be exalted with honour.

- *Pr 14:21*—He that despiseth his neighbour sinneth: but he that hath mercy on the poor, happy [is] he.

- *Pr 14:31*—He that oppresseth the poor reproacheth his Maker: but he that honoureth him hath mercy on the poor.

- *Pr 19:17*—He that hath pity upon the poor lendeth unto the LORD; and that which he hath given will he pay him again.

- *Pr 21:13*—Whoso stoppeth his ears at the cry of the poor, he also shall cry himself, but shall not be heard.

- *Pr 22:9*—He that hath a bountiful eye shall be blessed; for he giveth of his bread to the poor.

- *Pr 22:16*—He that oppresseth the poor to increase his [riches, and] he that giveth to the rich, [shall] surely [come] to want.

- *Pr 28:8*—He that by usury and unjust gain increaseth his substance, he shall gather it for him that will pity the poor.

- ***Pr 28:27**—He that giveth unto the poor shall not lack: but he that hideth his eyes shall have many a curse.*

- ***Pr 29:14**—The king that faithfully judgeth the poor, his throne shall be established for ever.*

- ***Pr 31:10**—Who can find a virtuous woman? For her price [is] far above rubies.*

- ***Pr 31:20**—She stretcheth out her hand to the poor; yea, she reacheth forth her hands to the needy.*

- ***Isa 1:16**—Wash you, make you clean; put away the evil of your doings from before mine eyes; cease to do evil; 17 Learn to do well; seek judgment, relieve the oppressed, judge the fatherless, plead for the widow.*

- ***Isa 1:23**—Thy princes [are] rebellious, and companions of thieves: every one loveth gifts, and followeth after rewards: they judge not the fatherless, neither doth the cause of the widow come unto them.*

- ***Isa 58:6**—Is not this the fast that I have chosen? To loose the bands of wickedness, to undo the heavy burdens, and to let the oppressed go free, and that ye break every yoke? 7 Is it not to deal thy bread to the hungry, and that thou bring the* *poor that are cast out to thy house? When thou seest the naked, that thou cover him; and that thou hide not thyself from thine own flesh? 8 Then shall thy light break forth as the morning, and thine health shall spring forth speedily: and thy righteousness shall go before thee; the glory of the LORD shall be thy reward. 9 Then shalt thou call, and the LORD shall answer; thou shalt cry, and he shall say, Here I am. If thou take away from the midst of thee the yoke, the putting forth of the finger, and speaking vanity; 10 And if thou draw out thy soul to the hungry, and satisfy the afflicted soul; then shall thy light rise in obscurity, and thy darkness be as the noonday: 11 And the LORD shall guide thee continually, and satisfy thy soul in drought, and make fat thy bones: and thou shalt be like a watered garden, and like a spring of water, whose waters fail not.*

- ***Jer 22:15**—Shalt thou reign, because thou closest thyself in cedar? Did not thy father eat and drink, and do judgment and justice, and then it was well with him? 16 He judged the cause of the poor and needy; then it was well with him: was not this to know me? saith the LORD. 17 But thine eyes and thine heart are not but for thy covetousness, and for to shed innocent blood, and for oppression, and for violence, to do it.*

- *Eze 16:49*—*Behold, this was the iniquity of thy sister Sodom, pride, fullness of bread, and abundance of idleness was in her and in her daughters, neither did she strengthen the hand of the poor and needy.*

- *Eze 22:29*—*The people of the land have used oppression, and exercised robbery, and have vexed the poor and needy: yea, they have oppressed the stranger wrongfully. 30 And I sought for a man among them, that should make up the hedge, and stand in the gap before me for the land, that I should not destroy it: but I found none.*

- *Eze 33:31*—*And they come unto thee as the people cometh, and they sit before thee [as] my people, and they hear thy words, but they will not do them: for with their mouth they shew much love, [but] their heart goeth after their covetousness.*

- *Da 4:27*—*Wherefore, O king, let my counsel be acceptable unto thee, and break off thy sins by righteousness, and thine iniquities by shewing mercy to the poor; if it may be a lengthening of thy tranquility.*

- *Amos 5:11*—*Forasmuch therefore as your treading is upon the poor, and ye take from him burdens of wheat: ye have built houses of hewn stone, but ye shall not dwell in them; ye have planted pleasant vineyards, but ye shall not drink wine of them. 12 For I know your manifold transgressions and your mighty sins: they afflict the just, they take a bribe, and they turn aside the poor in the gate from their right. 13 Therefore the prudent shall keep silence in that time; for it is an evil time. 14 Seek good, and not evil, that ye may live: and so the LORD, the God of hosts, shall be with you, as ye have spoken.*

- *Am 8:4—Hear this, O ye that swallow up the needy, even to make the poor of the land to fail.*

- *Am 8:6—That we may buy the poor for silver, and the needy for a pair of shoes; [yea], and sell the refuse of the wheat?*

- *Am 8:11—Behold, the days come, saith the Lord GOD, that I will send a famine in the land, not a famine of bread, nor a thirst for water, but of hearing the words of the LORD:*

- *Zech 7:9—Thus speaketh the LORD of hosts, saying, Execute true judgment, and shew mercy and compassions every man to his brother: 10 And oppress not the widow, nor the fatherless, the stranger, nor the poor; and let none of you imagine evil against his brother in your heart. 11 But they refused to hearken, and pulled away the shoulder, and stopped their ears, that they should not hear. 12 Yea, they made their hearts as an adamant stone, lest they should hear the law, and the words which the LORD of hosts hath sent in his spirit by the former prophets: therefore came a great wrath from the LORD of hosts.*

- **Mal 3:3**—*And he shall sit as a refiner and purifier of silver: and he shall purify the sons of Levi, and purge them as gold and silver, that they may offer unto the LORD an offering in righteousness. 4 Then shall the offering of Judah and Jerusalem be pleasant unto the LORD, as in the days of old, and as in former years. 5 And I will come near to you to judgment; and I will be a swift witness against the sorcerers, and against the adulterers, and against false swearers, and against those that oppress the hireling in his wages, the widow, and the fatherless, and that turn aside the stranger from his right, and fear not me, saith the LORD of hosts. 6 For I am the LORD, I change not; therefore ye sons of Jacob are not consumed. 7 Even from the days of your fathers ye are gone away from mine ordinances, and have not kept them. Return unto me, and I will return unto you, saith the LORD of hosts. But ye said, Wherein shall we return? 8 Will a man rob God? Yet ye have robbed me. But ye say, Wherein have we robbed thee? In tithes and offerings. 9 Ye are cursed with a curse: for ye have robbed me, even this whole nation. 10 Bring ye all the tithes into the storehouse, that there* *may be meat in mine house, and prove me now herewith, saith the LORD of hosts, if I will not open you the windows of heaven, and pour you out a blessing, that there shall not be room enough to receive it. 11 And I will rebuke the devourer for your sakes, and he shall not destroy the fruits of your ground; neither shall your vine cast her fruit before the time in the field, saith the LORD of hosts.*

- *Matt 6:1—Take heed that ye do not your alms before men, to be seen of them: otherwise ye have no reward of your Father which is in heaven. 2 Therefore when thou doest thine alms, do not sound a trumpet before thee, as the hypocrites do in the synagogues and in the streets, that they may have glory of men. Verily I say unto you, They have their reward. 3 But when thou doest alms, let not thy left hand know what thy right hand doeth: 3 That thine alms may be in secret: and thy Father which seeth in secret himself shall reward thee openly.*

- *Mt 19:20—The young man saith unto him, All these things have I kept from my youth up: what lack I yet?*

- *Mt 19:21—Jesus said unto him, If thou wilt be perfect, go [and] sell that thou hast, and give to the poor, and thou shalt have treasure in heaven: and come [and] follow me.*

- *Mt 25:34—Then shall the King say unto them on his right hand, Come, ye blessed of my Father, inherit the kingdom prepared for you from the foundation of the world: 35 For I was an hungered, and ye gave me meat: I was thirsty, and ye gave me drink: I was a stranger, and ye took me in: 36 Naked, and ye clothed me: I was sick, and ye visited me: I was in prison, and ye came unto me. 37 Then shall the righteous answer him, saying, Lord, when saw we thee an hungered, and fed thee? or thirsty, and gave thee drink? 38 When saw we thee a stranger, and took thee in? or naked, and clothed thee? 39 Or when saw we thee sick, or in prison, and came unto thee? 40 And the King shall answer and say unto them, Verily I say unto you, Inasmuch as ye have done it unto one of the least of these my brethren, ye have done it unto me. 41 Then shall he say also unto them on the left hand, Depart from me, ye cursed, into everlasting fire, prepared for the devil and his angels: 42 For I was an hungered, and ye gave me no meat: I was thirsty, and ye gave me no drink: 43 I was a stranger, and ye took me not in: naked, and ye clothed me not: sick, and in prison, and ye visited me not. 44 Then shall they also answer him, saying, Lord, when saw we thee an hungered, or athirst, or a stranger, or naked, or sick, or in prison, and did not minister unto thee? 45 Then shall he answer them, saying, Verily I say unto you, Inasmuch as ye did it not to one of the least of these, ye did it not to me.*

- **Luke 3:7**—*Then said he to the multitude that came forth to be baptized of him, O generation of vipers, who hath warned you to flee from the wrath to come? 8 Bring forth therefore fruits worthy of repentance, and begin not to say within yourselves, We have Abraham to our father: for I say unto you, That God is able of these stones to raise up children unto Abraham. 9 And now also the axe is laid unto the root of the trees: every tree therefore which bringeth not forth good fruit is hewn down, and cast into the fire. 10 And the people asked him, saying, What shall we do then? 11 He answereth and saith unto them, He that hath two coats, let him impart to him that hath none; and he that hath meat, let him do likewise.*

- **Luke 6:30**—*Give to every man that asketh of thee; and of him that taketh away thy goods ask them not again. 31 And as ye would that men should do to you, do ye also to them likewise. 32 For if ye love them which love you, what thank have ye? for sinners also love those that love them. 33 And if ye do good to them which do good to you, what thank have ye? for sinners also do even the same. 34 And if ye lend to them of whom ye hope to receive, what thank have ye? for sinners also lend to sinners, to receive as much again. 35 But love ye your enemies, and do* *good, and lend, hoping for nothing again; and your reward shall be great, and ye shall be the children of the Highest: for he is kind unto the unthankful and to the evil. 36 Be ye therefore merciful, as your Father also is merciful. 37 Judge not, and ye shall not be judged: condemn not, and ye shall not be condemned: forgive, and ye shall be forgiven: 38 Give, and it shall be given unto you; good measure, pressed down, and shaken together, and running over, shall men give into your bosom. For with the same measure that ye mete withal it shall be measured to you again.*

- *Luke 10:33—But a certain Samaritan, as he journeyed, came where he was: and when he saw him, he had compassion on him, 34 And went to him, and bound up his wounds, pouring in oil and wine, and set him on his own beast, and brought him to an inn, and took care of him. 35 And on the morrow when he departed, he took out two pence, and gave them to the host, and said unto him, Take care of him; and whatsoever thou spendest more, when I come again, I will repay thee. 36 Which now of these three, thinkest thou, was neighbour unto him that fell among the thieves? 37 And he said, He that shewed mercy on him. Then said Jesus unto him, Go, and do thou likewise.*

- *Luke 11:39—And the Lord said unto him, Now do ye Pharisees make clean the outside of the cup and the platter; but your inward part is full of ravening and wickedness. 40 Ye fools, did not he that made that which is without make that which is within also? 41 But rather give alms of such things as ye have; and, behold, all things are clean unto you.*

- *Luke 12:20—But God said unto him, Thou fool, this night thy soul shall be required of thee: then whose shall those things be, which thou hast provided? 21 So is he that layeth up treasure for himself, and is not rich toward God. 31 But rather seek ye the kingdom of God; and all these things shall be added unto you. 32 Fear not, little flock; for it is your Father's good pleasure to give you the kingdom. 33 Sell that ye have, and give alms; provide yourselves bags which wax not old, a treasure in the heavens that faileth not, where no thief approacheth, neither moth corrupteth. 34 For where your treasure is, there will your heart be also.*

- *Luke 14:12—Then said he also to him that bade him, When thou makest a dinner or a supper, call not thy friends, nor thy brethren, neither thy kinsmen, nor thy rich neighbours; lest they also bid thee again, and a recompence be made thee. 13 But when thou makest a feast, call the poor, the maimed, the lame, the blind: 13 And thou shalt be blessed; for they cannot recompense thee: for thou shalt be recompensed at the resurrection of the just.*

- **Luke 14:21**—*So that servant came, and shewed his lord these things. Then the master of the house being angry said to his servant, Go out quickly into the streets and lanes of the city, and bring in hither the poor, and the maimed, and the halt, and the blind. 22 And the servant said, Lord, it is done as thou hast commanded, and yet there is room. 23 And the lord said unto the servant, Go out into the highways and hedges, and compel them to come in, that my house may be filled.*

- **Luke 16:19**—*There was a certain rich man, which was clothed in purple and fine linen, and fared sumptuously every day: 20 And there was a certain beggar named Lazarus, which was laid at his gate, full of sores, 21 And desiring to be fed with the crumbs which fell from the rich man's table: moreover the dogs came and licked his sores. 22 And it came to pass, that the beggar died, and was carried by the angels into Abraham's bosom: the rich man also died, and was buried; 23 And in hell he lift up his eyes, being in torments, and seeth Abraham afar off, and Lazarus in his bosom. 31 And he said unto him, If they hear not Moses and the prophets, neither will they be persuaded, though one rose from the dead.*

- *Luke 19:5—And when Jesus came to the place, he looked up, and saw him, and said unto him, Zacchaeus, make haste, and come down; for to day I must abide at thy house. 6 And he made haste, and came down, and received him joyfully. 7 And when they saw it, they all murmured, saying, That he was gone to be guest with a man that is a sinner. 8 And Zacchaeus stood, and said unto the Lord; Behold, Lord, the half of my goods I give to the poor; and if I have taken any thing from any man by false accusation, I restore him fourfold. 9 And Jesus said unto him, This day is salvation come to this house, forsomuch as he also is a son of Abraham.*

- *John 13:28—Now no man at the table knew for what intent he spake this unto him. 29 For some of them thought, because Judas had the bag, that Jesus had said unto him, Buy those things that we have need of against the feast; or, that he should give something to the poor.*

- *Acts 2:42—And they continued steadfastly in the apostles' doctrine and fellowship, and in breaking of bread, and in prayers. 43 And fear came upon every soul: and many wonders and signs were done by the apostles. 44 And all that believed were together, and had all things common; 45 And sold their possessions and goods, and parted them to all men, as every man had need.*

- *Acts 4:32*—And the multitude of them that believed were of one heart and of one soul: neither said any of them that ought of the things which he possessed was his own; but they had all things common. 33 And with great power gave the apostles witness of the resurrection of the Lord Jesus: and great grace was upon them all. 34 Neither was there any among them that lacked: for as many as were possessors of lands or houses sold them, and brought the prices of the things that were sold, 35 And laid them down at the apostles' feet: and distribution was made unto every man according as he had need.

- *Acts 6:1*—And in those days, when the number of the disciples was multiplied, there arose a murmuring of the Grecians against the Hebrews, because their widows were neglected in the daily ministration. 2 Then the twelve called the multitude of the disciples unto them, and said, It is not reason that we should leave the word of God, and serve tables. 4 Wherefore, brethren, look ye out among you seven men of honest report, full of the Holy Ghost and wisdom, whom we may appoint over this business.

- *Acts 9:36*—Now there was at Joppa a certain disciple named Tabitha, which by interpretation is called Dorcas: this woman was full of good works and alms deeds which she did.

- *Acts 10:1—There was a certain man in Caesarea called Cornelius, a centurion of the band called the Italian band, 2 A devout man, and one that feared God with all his house, which gave much alms to the people, and prayed to God always. 3 He saw in a vision evidently about the ninth hour of the day an angel of God coming in to him, and saying unto him, Cornelius. 4 And when he looked on him, he was afraid, and said, What is it, Lord? And he said unto him, Thy prayers and thine alms are come up for a memorial before God. 30 And Cornelius said, Four days ago I was fasting until this hour; and at the ninth hour I prayed in my house, and, behold, a man stood before me in bright clothing, 31 And said, Cornelius, thy prayer is heard, and thine alms are had in remembrance in the sight of God.*

- *Acts 20:33—I have coveted no man's silver, or gold, or apparel. 34 Yea, ye yourselves know, that these hands have ministered unto my necessities, and to them that were with me. 35 I have shewed you all things, how that so labouring ye ought to support the weak, and to remember the words of the Lord Jesus, how he said, It is more blessed to give than to receive.*

- *Rom 12:14—Distributing to the necessity of saints; given to hospitality. 20 Therefore if thine enemy hunger, feed him; if he thirst, give him* drink: for in so doing thou shalt heap coals of fire on his head. 21 Be not overcome of evil, but overcome evil with good.

- **II Cor 8:13**—For I mean not that other men be eased, and ye burdened: 14 But by an equality, that now at this time your abundance may be a supply for their want, that their abundance also may be a supply for your want: that there may be equality: 15 As it is written, He that had gathered much had nothing over; and he that had gathered little had no lack.

- **II Cor 9:1**—For as touching the ministering to the saints, it is superfluous for me to write to you: 8 And God is able to make all grace abound toward you; that ye, always having all sufficiency in all things, may abound to every good work: 9 (As it is written, He hath dispersed abroad; he hath given to the poor: his righteousness remaineth forever. 10 Now he that ministereth seed to the sower both minister bread for your food, and multiply your seed sown, and increase the fruits of your righteousness;) 11 Being enriched in every thing to all bountifulness, which causeth through us thanksgiving to God. 12 For the administration of this service not only supplieth the want of the saints, but is abundant also by many thanksgivings unto God; 13 Whiles by the experiment of this ministration they glorify God for your professed subjection unto the *gospel of Christ, and for your liberal distribution unto them, and unto all men;*

- *Gal 2:9—And when James, Cephas, and John, who seemed to be pillars, perceived the grace that was given unto me, they gave to me and Barnabas the right hands of fellowship; that we should go unto the heathen, and they unto the circumcision. 10 Only they would that we should remember the poor; the same which I also was forward to do.*

- *Eph 4:28—Let him that stole steal no more: but rather let him labour, working with his hands the thing which is good, that he may have to give to him that needeth.*

- *I Tim 5:16—If any man or woman that believeth have widows, let them relieve them, and let not the church be charged; that it may relieve them that are widows indeed.*

- *I Tim 6:17—Charge them that are rich in this world, that they be not high-minded, nor trust in uncertain riches, but in the living God, who giveth us richly all things to enjoy; 18 That they do good, that they be rich in good works, ready to distribute, willing to communicate; 18 Laying up in store for themselves a good foundation against the time to come, that they may lay hold on eternal life.*

- *James 1:27—Pure religion and undefiled before God and the Father is this, To visit the fatherless and widows in their affliction, and to keep himself unspotted from the world.*

- *James 2:1—My brethren, have not the faith of our Lord Jesus Christ, the Lord of glory, with respect of persons. 2 For if there come unto your assembly a man with a gold ring, in goodly apparel, and there come in also a poor man in vile raiment; 3 And ye have respect to him that weareth the gay clothing, and say unto him, Sit thou here in a good place; and say to the poor, Stand thou there, or sit here under my footstool: 4 Are ye not then partial in yourselves, and are become judges of evil thoughts? 5 Hearken, my beloved brethren, Hath not God chosen the poor of this world rich in faith, and heirs of the kingdom which he hath promised to them that love him? 6 But ye have despised the poor. Do not rich men oppress you, and draw you before the judgment seats? 7 Do not they blaspheme that worthy name by which ye are called? 8 If ye fulfill the royal law according to the scripture, Thou shalt love thy neighbour as thyself, ye do well: 14 What doth it profit, my brethren, though a man say he hath faith, and have not works? Can faith save him? 15 If a brother or sister be naked, and destitute of daily food, 16And one of you say unto them, Depart in peace, be ye warmed and filled; notwithstanding ye give them*

*not those things which are needful to the body;
what doth it profit? 17 Even so faith, if it hath not
works, is dead, being alone.*

- *I Jn 3:16*—*Hereby perceive we the love of God,
because he laid down his life for us: and we
ought to lay down our lives for the brethren. 17
But whoso hath this world's good, and seeth his
brother have need, and shutteth up his bowels of
compassion from him, how dwelleth the love of
God in him? 19 My little children, let us not love
in word, neither in tongue; but in deed and in
truth.*

Good Works

- *II Tim 3:16*—*All scripture is given by inspiration
of God, and is profitable for doctrine, for
reproof, for correction, for instruction in
righteousness: 17 That the man of God may be
perfect, thoroughly furnished unto all good
works.*

- *Titus 2:14*—*Who gave himself for us, that he
might redeem us from all iniquity, and purify
unto himself a peculiar people, zealous of good
works.*

- *Titus 3:8*—*This is a faithful saying, and these
things I will that thou affirm constantly, that they
which have believed in God might be careful to*

maintain good works. These things are good and profitable unto men.

- *Heb 10:24—And let us consider one another to provoke unto love and to good works: 25 Not forsaking the assembling of ourselves together, as the manner of some is; but exhorting one another: and so much the more, as ye see the day approaching.*

About The Author

Rick has been a Founding and Head Pastor for over 18 years, the last 12 years at Ponce Church in Ponce Inlet, FL.

"One of the five best Bible teachers in the world", according to Dr. Kevin McNulty, World Missions Director and Founder of Christian Adventures International, Daytona Beach, FL.

An instructor in 3 different Bible schools, mission trip organizer, equipping and facilitating others to accept their call to ministry or mission.

As a young man, God called Rick to "spend his time in ministry and the Word" and since that call, he has spent over 30,000 hours in the study of scripture.

Rick's greatest accomplishment: currently feeding over 150 meals every week to our homeless friends on North St. in Daytona Beach, FL.

About SermonToBook.Com

SermonToBook.com began with a simple belief: that sermons should be touching lives, *not* collecting dust. That's why we turn sermons into high-quality books that are accessible to people all over the globe.

Turning your sermon or sermon series into a book exposes more people to God's Word, better equips you for counseling, accelerates future sermon prep, adds credibility to your ministry, and even helps make ends meet during tight times.

John 21:25 tells us that the world itself couldn't contain the books that would be written about the work of Jesus Christ. Our mission is to try anyway. Because, in Heaven, there will no longer be a need for sermons or books. Our time is now.

If God so leads you, we'd love to work with you on your sermon or sermon series.

Visit www.sermontobook.com to learn more.

Encourage the Author by Reviewing This Book

If you've found this book helpful or challenging, the author would love your honest feedback. Please consider stopping by Amazon.com and writing a review.

To submit a review, simply go to this book's Amazon.com page, click "Write a customer review" in the Customer Reviews section, and click submit.

Made in the USA
Charleston, SC
25 May 2015